BUILDING WITHIN NATURE

Books by Andy and Sally Wasowski

Gardening with Native Plants of the South
Gardening with Prairie Plants
The Landscaping Revolution
Native Landscaping from El Paso to L.A.
Native Texas Gardens
Native Texas Plants
Requiem for a Lawnmower

Building within Nature

A Guide for Home Owners, Contractors, and Architects

Andy Wasowski

with Sally Wasowski

Foreword by Darrel G. Morrison, FASLA

Photography by Andy Wasowski

University of Minnesota Press
Minneapolis • London

Originally published in hardcover as *Building Inside Nature's Envelope:
How New Construction and Land Preservation Can Work Together*
by Oxford University Press, Inc.

First University of Minnesota Press edition, 2006

Published by the University of Minnesota Press
111 Third Avenue South, Suite 290
Minneapolis, MN 55401-2520
http://www.upress.umn.edu

Printed in China on acid-free paper

Library of Congress Cataloging-in-Publication Data

Wasowski, Andy, 1939–
      [Building inside nature's envelope]
      Building within nature : a guide for home owners, contractors, and architects / Andy
Wasowski with Sally Wasowski ; foreword by Darrel G. Morrison ; photography by Andy
Wasowski. — 1st ed.
          p.   cm.
      Originally published: Building inside nature's envelope. Oxford, UK ; New York :
Oxford University Press, 2000.
      Includes bibliographical references and index.
      ISBN-13: 978-0-816-64902-0 (pb : alk. paper)
      ISBN-10: 0-8166-4902-2 (pb : alk. paper)
      1. House construction—Environmental aspects. 2. Landscape architecture—
Environmental aspects. I. Wasowski, Sally, 1946– II. Title.
      TH4812.W36 2006
      720'.47—dc22

                                                                                    2005029151

The University of Minnesota is an equal-opportunity educator and employer.

14 13 12 11 10 09 08 07 06   10 9 8 7 6 5 4 3 2 1

In memory of my dad, Boleslaw Wasowski

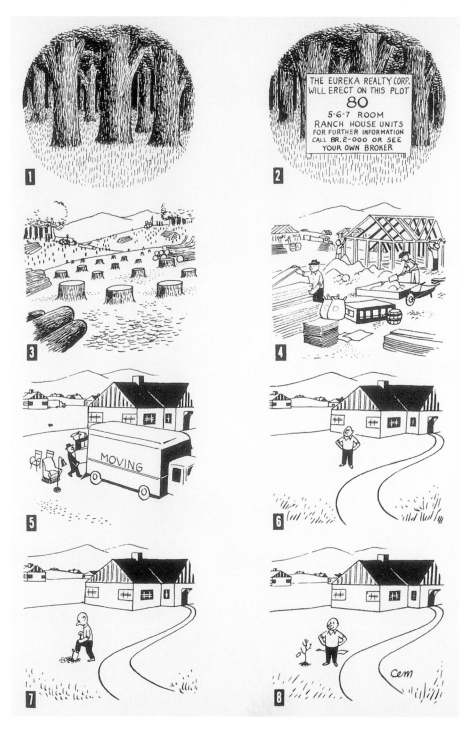

How many people were thinking about the environment back in the early 1950s? Cartoonist Charles E. Martin was surely ahead of his time when he showed us all too graphically what was—and still is—common practice in new home construction. (©Charles E. Martin)

Contents

Foreword

As I write this, I have just spent three weeks immersed in a variety of natural or seminatural landscapes in the southeastern United States: the beaches and dunes, maritime live oak forests, and salt marshes of Cumberland Island, off the coast of Georgia; the longleaf pines/wiregrass savannas and pitcher plant bogs of the coastal plain; the upland and floodplain forests and granitic outcrops of Georgia's central piedmont; and the forested coves, slopes, and ridges of the north Georgia mountains, as well as spruce-fir forests and grassy balds over a mile high in elevation in the southern Appalachians of North Carolina.

The occasion for this nearly total immersion in such a rich array of field sites was to coteach a course entitled "Native Plant Communities of the Southeast," to a group of fifteen University of Georgia students of landscape architecture and ecology or, more accurately, to learn with them more about the complex natural landscapes of the region as models for our own work in designing, restoring, and managing landscapes.

As is always the case when I have the opportunity to study the aesthetic and botanic composition, ecological interactions, and dynamics of natural communities, I have been reinspired by the fitness and function of native vegetation matched with its environment and the elegant, unique beauty that ensues. Among the images that are indelibly imprinted in my memory of this most recent field trip are the following: a late afternoon backlit vista of vertical longleaf pine trunks in a vividly green sea of wiregrass, wildflowers, and ferns near Moultrie, Georgia; the gnarled spreading branches of live oak trees silhouetted against an azure sky, draped with swaying Spanish moss, with dense patches of saw palmettos beneath them on Cumberland Island; the luxuriant flowering of pink mountain laurel and orange flame azaleas on the slopes of Blood Mountain; the wind-rippled mountain oat grass, hairgrass, and hay-scented ferns going to the horizon on a high-elevation grassy bald in North Carolina.

But even as I was inspired and enthralled with the beauty and fitness of these distinctive naturally evolved and human-protected landscapes, my rapture was tempered by the knowledge that every day other biotically rich and aesthetically rewarding landscapes—even on seemingly remote mountainsides and barrier islands—are being lost to bulldozers and short-sighted "development," to be replaced far too often by highly simplified or even dysfunctional landscapes that resemble too closely our generic, homogeneous suburbs.

The knowledge that this is happening prompts two responses. First, it emphasizes the need to practice stewardship of increasingly rare landscapes and species through outright preservation—exhibiting some of the spirit and vision of our predecessors who had the foresight to protect many of the natural areas we studied as a class these past three weeks. Second, when we choose to develop sites that possess natural diversity and beauty, we need to practice on-site stewardship by minimizing the amount of disruption of that diversity and beauty.

Which brings us to the subject of Andy Wasowski's book, *Building Inside Nature's Envelope*. Essentially, the concept Wasowski espouses is one that conscientious site planners and landscape architects have traditionally applied. Unfortunately, a headlong rush for expediency, combined with a lack of awareness or appreciation of the values of protecting the native vegetation, topography, and unique character of a site has led to the unnecessary loss of biotic diversity and natural beauty in far too many built-upon landscapes.

In this book, Andy lays out, in straightforward fashion and easily understandable terms, the logic of and methods for minimizing disruption of natural systems when we build on the land. Furthermore, throughout his discussion and the case studies he cites, he shows that the minimum disruption scenario can be a win-win solution. Not only does the environment benefit from the careful planning and construction methods that protect functioning natural communities, but humans who occupy the resultant landscape benefit as well. We benefit from the shading and cooling effects provided by mature trees, from the natural erosion control provided by an intact ground layer of woodland or grassland herbaceous plant species, and the very real economic savings that are derived from not having to revegetate large areas or "landscape" it in a traditional sense.

But the biggest bonus of all may be less obvious than the above clearly practical benefits: looking out the window of a house or an office or a schoolroom and seeing a landscape that is truly "of the place" within a few feet of the building, or finding joy in the knowledge that we humans can live in harmony with our natural surroundings and with other forms of life.

The rationale, the techniques, and the examples of building within nature's envelope that are covered in this book will, I hope, reach a broad audience who will, one way or another, affect the landscapes we collectively occupy: homeowners, builders, professional engineers and site planners, school board and corporate board members, to name a few. In fact, everyone could benefit from a widespread adoption of the ideas outlined in these pages.

Darrel G. Morrison, FASLA

Acknowledgments

Things are always falling through the proverbial cracks. No question about it, there is information I had that somehow never made it into these pages. One day, I'll be looking through the published book and I'll slap my forehead and lament that a perfectly good statistic or case history was inexplicably omitted. I know this happens to all authors, but it's disconcerting nonetheless.

This kind of mental lapse is especially troubling in the acknowledgments. Since this is my eighth book, you would think that getting at least this part right should be a snap for me by now. Trouble is, there was no clearly defined starting point for this book; Sally and I were collecting information on the envelope long before we had even considered doing a book. Research and interviews took place over many years, often at times when we were busily involved in other projects, and we didn't always keep scrupulous notes on all contributors. Or names were hastily scribbled on slips of paper that mysteriously wound up in the twilight zone. So—if your name is among the missing, please know that your input was no less valuable or appreciated. Among the many helpful people we have managed to recall are Debra Allen, Phil Anderson, Steve Aphelbaum, Sarah Beyer, Jack Broughton, Tamara Graham Calabria, Gage Davis, Harvey Durham, Wade Elston, Christy Gibson,

Randy Harelson, Diana Herbert, Marcia Herman, Cindy Hollar, Kevin Hornick, Lynn Hudson, Lisa Gundelfinger, John P. Gutting, Walter Johanson, Wanda Jones, Kevin Kelly, John Knott, Jared Martin, Scott Martin, Nirmalan and Komalam Mayura, Stephen Merdler, Ann Moore, Carl Ohlandt, Linda Overbaugh, Michael Pawlukiewicz, Michael Parkey, Monica Ann Pesek, Clinton Piper, Robert Poore, Gene Powell, Albee Richardson, Leslie Sauer, Harold Spiegel, Dick and Mary Stanley, Kevin Tennison, and Bill Wiemeyer.

And special thanks to our agent, Jeanne Fredericks, for her faith in this project and her hard work in getting it off the ground.

Introduction

In March of 1991, the National Wildflower Research Center (since renamed the Lady Bird Johnson Wildflower Center) and the Desert Botanical Garden in Phoenix co-sponsored a native plant seminar in Mesa, Arizona. Although I was unable to attend, my wife Sally went in her capacity as a professional landscape designer. When she returned home, one of the first things she said to me was, "Guess what? It has a name!"

"It" was an exciting new technique for building homes in natural areas while still preserving the natural ecosystem. It was a technique we had become acquainted with several years earlier when we met Gerald and Rosalie Cyrier, who had built their new home on a half-acre tract of Eastern Cross Timbers, a vegetational region in northern Texas, and managed to save over 80 percent of the woodland. At that time, neither we nor the Cyriers knew that what they had done had a name.

Sally told me that the speaker, Ivan Broman, manager of architectural design for a development company in Scottsdale, had called this technique "the building envelope" and had presented it as a detailed, step-by-step process as used at Desert Mountain, an 8,000-acre master-planned community in north Scottsdale that abutted the Tonto National Forest.

The approach that the Cyriers used wasn't nearly as involved. They simply

"When some remote ancestor invented the shovel, he became a giver. He could plant a tree. And when the axe was invented he became a taker. He could chop it down. Whoever owns land has thus assumed, whether he knows it or not, the divine functions of creating and destroying plants."

—Aldo Leopold
Sand County Almanac

Tucked into this Eastern Cross Timbers landscape in Bedford, Texas, is the home of Gerald and Rosalie Cyrier, the first people we met who had actually used the "envelope" technique in preserving their native woodland. They didn't know this approach had a name, but they understood its importance.

told their builder to stay out of the woods—which consisted of native post oaks, blackjack oaks, American elms, and red mulberries, and a carpet of native Virginia creeper—and preserve as much of the vegetation around the building site as possible.

Since the Cyriers had purchased one of ten similar lots and were the first to build on it, they had hoped they'd be setting a good example for their neighbors-to-be. Unfortunately, when the other lots were sold, the new owners cut down most of the trees and installed conventional lawns. (An interesting sidelight: At that time, Gerald Cyrier was a lawnmower salesman!)

Broman's presentation, coupled with the example of the Cyriers' home, prompted me to look for other builders and homeowners using this technique—no matter what they called it. In fact, I was later to learn that the term "building envelope," although used by at least half of the people I'd encountered, may be a misnomer. One architect informed me that "building envelope" designates the outer wall of a structure, and has nothing to do with the property surrounding the building. It was certainly not used in any landscaping sense. As used at Desert Mountain, the term means the maximum allowable building area on each lot—out to but not entering the natural area being preserved. The term envelope comes from the fact that the natural area envelops the building site, or "footprint." Some architects and builders I met referred to building inside a natural perimeter or boundary; architect Richard Meier refers to it as an enclosure.

Whatever it was called, before very long I was discovering numerous examples—both single homes and entire developments—of this environmentally friendly building approach. They were in all parts of the country, on all sorts of terrain, from woodlands to deserts to savannas to coastal scrub—and in greater numbers than I had initially expected. Still, it became clear that these examples constituted a very small percentage of all the construction going on across the country—including in natural areas. And the vast majority of people in the building professions, not to mention average homeowners, knew nothing of this technique.

Having a touch of the missionary in me, I wrote a few articles on the subject—not because I was an authority, but because no one else seemed to be doing it, and I felt that people needed to know about this option. Inexplicably, I found no interest in this subject at the "environmental" publications I queried. I can only guess that they misunderstood the concept and must have thought I was encouraging people to build in natural areas that would otherwise remain pristine. This of course is not true; the natural areas I am addressing are going to be built on. The question is, will they be built on in an environmentally responsible manner, or with conventional land-*scraping* methods?

As word of the envelope got around, I was invited to give slide presentations on the envelope, and I introduced it to garden clubs, native plant societies, Master Gardeners, and even the Dallas chapter of the Sierra Club. In each instance I was amazed at how enthusiastically news of this technique was received. I knew that most members of the audience would probably never have need for this information themselves, yet they were excited that such a commonsense alternative to bulldozing was available and being used, albeit sparsely. This positive reception indicated that a book on the subject would not be a terrible idea. The information would, I felt, be especially valuable to students of architecture, landscape architecture, landscape design, urban planning, and the environmental sciences.

If *Building Inside Nature's Envelope* helps to inspire a more positive attitude toward conservation within the building community, the legislative bodies of this country, and the general public, then it was worth doing. It was never my intention to make this book a highly complex technical manual or academic textbook. This would have rendered it inaccessible to a vast audience of laypeople who will also want to be aware of this option. Instead, it is intended to serve as an easily accessible eye-opener, a basic introduction to what a growing number of people are seeing as an exciting and sensible alternative to traditional land-scraping methods.

Besides, complexity is unnecessary. Nature's envelope is simple to understand and easy to execute. The technique requires just two things: a situation that allows this approach to be utilized, and the willingness of the builder or property owner to try it. I've talked to a number of builders who, after having successfully completed their first envelope project, are enthusiastic converts—for bottom line as well as environmental reasons.

In the first few decades of this new millennium, we will all become more environmentally aware. We will have no choice. The consequences of dwindling and threatened resources, endangered plant and animal species, and our escalating world population—the root cause of virtually all our environmental problems—will become too manifest to be ignored except by the most mindless individuals. And, I firmly believe, during this time, the envelope will become an important part of our response to the environmental problems that beset us.

BUILDING WITHIN NATURE

↔ Keep Nature at Arm's Length ↔ 1

We appear to be changing directions.

Beginning after the Civil War, there was a major exodus out of rural America, where opportunities ranged from few to nonexistent, and into urban areas where people sought jobs, educational opportunities, and "the good life." Today, urban and suburban crime, congestion, pollution, and a skyrocketing cost of living are causing a large number of people to reevaluate their definition of the good life and to begin packing.

As a result, every year, many thousands of acres of natural land—woodlands, deserts, meadowlands, savannas, coastal scrub—are turned into homesites by disenchanted city dwellers and by developers eager to tap into this ready market of expatriates. Ironically, by the time the moving vans pull up to many of these newly completed homes, the beauty and character of the land—the very things that attracted the buyers in the first place—have been harmed or destroyed. Bulldozers have scraped the land clean of all vegetation, in many cases leveling the lots so that all traces of the original topographical features—arroyos, slopes, rock outcroppings, etc.—have been eradicated.

After these homes are completed, the properties are relandscaped, most often with standard nursery stock that has little or nothing to do with what had grown

"We do not live apart from nature, we are a part of nature."

—Bret Rappaport, Environmental Attorney

More than ever, people are escaping the rigors of life in urban and suburban areas and are seeking the "good life" in more natural locales. Some areas are fairly remote, as here in the foothills of the Sangre de Cristo Mountains of northern New Mexico. But others are relatively close to "civilization." Untouched natural areas can even be found on undeveloped lots in suburban neighborhoods.

there originally. The properties end up sporting lawns, box hedges, and lots of exotic bedding plants such as begonias, impatiens, hostas, and marigolds. In the end, these "homes in the wilderness" look like they could fit into any typical suburban neighborhood.

Why does this happen? There are two main reasons. First, these new homes are built using traditional building methods that put the construction first and the land second. Typical builders do not necessarily think of themselves as antienvironmentalists; it's just that their job is to build new homes, not protect habitats. They see their responsibility as completing the house on time and on budget. Period. We are, after all, a very bottom-line oriented society, and the vegetation and topography on the lot can often be viewed as impediments to efficiency. One builder I encountered actually bulldozed a dozen trees on his job site just to provide more parking space for his subcontractors.

In many cases, a builder or developer will allow a select number of shade trees to remain—as long as they are off to the side and out of his way. But frequently this has more to do with marketing than environmental concerns. Homes with shade trees are desirable, and will attract buyers faster than homes with denuded lots or a few saplings installed at the last minute.

In any case, many of these trees wind up dead or dying a year or so after move-in, the result of being girdled by heavy equipment; of being suffocated by dirt that is heaped up over the tree's flare at the base of the trunk, or being poisoned by the paints and the washout from cement mixers getting down into the root system.

These are common practices, and it isn't at all unusual to see evidence of all three on one job site.

The second reason for the destruction of natural home sites is the homeowners themselves. When they purchase a lot and then contract with a builder, they allow it to happen because they don't realize that they have any options. They consent to the clearing of their lot—assuming that they were even asked—because the builder tells them that's the way it has to be done. They accept this explanation because they have seen many other homes under construction, and those lots were also leveled and cleared.

What they probably hadn't considered is that, aside from the tragic environmental loss, there is a real dollars-and-cents value to all that natural vegetation. Moreover, they have already paid for it. The established landscape was a major factor in the original evaluation of the property. If they had seen it denuded of vegetation, the price would assuredly have been much lower. But then they would not have even considered buying it.

Look at it this way: You purchase a new car. Fully loaded. But before you pick it up, the dealer yanks out the stereo, the heater, the A/C, and the headrests. Would anyone seriously consider accepting the car in that condition? You'd hit the ceiling! Yet people docilely accept "delivery" on scraped land all the time.

THE OTHER COST

Although the cost of revegetating the property once the construction has been completed is high (as I demonstrate in chapter 5) permitting this wanton destruction is even more costly from an environmental perspective.

The sad fact is that public opinion polls still rank environmental considerations

This once lush woodland is being scraped clean to make way for a new subdivision. Conventional building practices clear and level the property so that the builders can have a "clean canvas" on which to work. Wildlife is displaced and homeowners have lost a mature, established, and low-maintenance landscape.

A healthy woodland once stood here. It has been replaced by a few saplings that are decades away from providing the shade, beauty, and habitat their predecessors had given. Yet, with a little creative thinking and preplanning, much of the woodland could have been saved.

low on the list of what matters most to us. And that is largely because the average citizen is simply not well versed in the basics of our natural world. When I was in school back in the 1950s, I recall learning how to dissect a frog in biology class and having to memorize (for as long as it took to pass the test, at which point all was lost!) the order, genus, and phylum of a dozen or so other critters. But I have no memory of ever being taught how they all interacted in the environment or why that was even important. Today, I wonder if my teachers even knew.

When a property has been scraped clean, a once thriving ecosystem has been destroyed, the established native vegetation—some of it endangered—has been lost, and countless forms of wildlife have been displaced. And for too many of us, that is essentially meaningless information.

Educator Lewis Thomas wrote, "The only solid piece of scientific truth about which I feel totally confident is that we are profoundly ignorant about nature." If you think he was being a bit harsh, consider the following examples:

❋ A 1996 poll conducted by the National Zoological Park in Washington, D.C., revealed that over 75 percent of visitors did not know the purpose of pollination. They certainly had no idea that most of our food—fruits, vegetables, grains—results from pollination and that there is a frightening worldwide decline in pollinators due largely to our overuse of pesticides.

❋ The parents at a Wisconsin elementary school were asked to approve the planting of a natural landscape on the property. The parents resoundingly said no! Their reason ... rabbits might jump out and scare the kids.

❊ Nurseries all over the country are selling many highly invasive exotic plants such as Chinese tallow, Australian eucalyptus, tamarisk, Brazilpepper, and Norway maple, to name just a few. These interlopers, lacking the natural controls (predators and parasites) that hold them in check in their native habitats, run amok here and outcompete the many native species that once grew in the same area. Instead of healthy biodiversity, we are left with sterile monocultures in which native plants and wildlife cannot flourish. Janet Marinelli, writing in her book *Invasive Plants*, calls these aliens "the true weeds of the modern world."

❊ Our federal government and state highway departments actually distribute invasive trees—Russian olive and Siberian elm—to ranchers in the Dakotas and Montana to be used as windbreaks. These trees now infest waterways from Canada to Texas. And if you think "infest" is too strong a word, I suggest you drive New Mexico state highway 64 from Blanco to Farmington. Russian olives clog the riverbanks in such numbers that one has to search diligently to spot the occasional native cottonwood or willow.

❊ In the 1920s, Kudzu, an Asian import, was distributed by government agencies to be used for erosion control. Kudzu is now referred to as "the vine that ate the South."

❊ A major company relocated its corporate headquarters near the Dallas/Fort Worth Airport in Texas. The original idea was sound—preserve the forest of mesquites on the property, along with the bluebonnets and other wildflowers that grew profusely among the trees. But once the building was

One of the most serious environmental problems we have in this country is also one of the least known. Invasive exotics, which lack the natural controls that kept them in check in their native ranges, are crowding out native vegetation and causing great harm to our natural habitats. Here, government-supplied Russian olives are being used as windbreaks around Dakota and Montana ranches.

Once distributed by govern-
ment agencies for erosion control,
kudzu is now known as the vine
that ate the South.

erected, this company installed a sprinkler system, not realizing that it had a naturally *xeriscapic* landscape, that is, one that could survive on rainfall alone. Before long the wildflowers drowned and have never come back.

NATURE AS A FOREIGN LAND

For many—especially young people growing up in urban and suburban neighborhoods—nature isn't relevant. In *The Geography of Childhood: Why Children Need Wild Places*, the authors relate the story of a PBS interview following the 1992 riots in Los Angeles. "One adolescent in south-central L.A. listed a half-dozen different automatic weapons used on the streets, and he was able to identify each by its sound.... These were the sounds he heard, learned, and sensed to be vital to his own existence. In another time or place, he would have spoken as matter-of-factly about the calls of six common species of hawks and owls."

For many of today's kids, a meadow or a patch of woods is unfamiliar territory, as mysterious as the back alleys of the Casbah. They are far more comfortable in, say, a video arcade or shopping mall. Put this in the dire category, because *especially* today it's hard to think of anything more relevant to our—and their—future than an understanding of and a respect for nature. Our continued existence on this planet depends on it. Simply put, what we don't know could ultimately do us in.

But people who are indifferent to or distrustful of nature are not easily convinced of this. They hear on the news that the spotted owl is threatened and their response is, "So what? We're doing okay without the dodo and the passenger pigeon!" Tell them that we are losing forests and woodlands at an alarming rate, and they will tell you about the last time they were in an airplane: "I looked down and saw zillions of trees. So what's all the fuss?"

This is how most of our children view nature—vicariously—on TV or in videos. Even a trip to the zoo is a poor substitute for the hands-on experience of hiking through a woodland or meadow, learning to identify native flora, collecting rocks or leaves, watching a mother bird feed her nestlings, or following the metamorphosis of a caterpillar into a butterfly. The environmental future of our planet is literally in the hands of our young, and they'd better be up to the job.

Of course, there are many others who are neither fearful of nature nor indifferent to it. These folks think that nature is swell and every so often pack the kids in the car and venture out into the country to see it. The idea that nature could—and should—exist right around their own homes, however, is as alien to them as mowing a lawn would be to a Kalahari bushman.

For the most part, we've lost contact with nature. In his book *The Value of Life*, Stephen Kellert points out that "for the majority of Americans, the vicarious experience of ... zoos, film, television, and other indirect means remains the predominant basis for encountering nature and living diversity."

Drive through any typical American neighborhood, virtually anywhere in the country, and the landscapes alone will show you how much we have separated ourselves from nature. Where in nature do we see plants lined up in perfect rows? Where in nature do we see shrubs that look like mushrooms and lollipops? Where in nature do you find grasses mowed into boot camp-style crewcuts?

The headline of an ad for Home Depot boldly sounds the call to action: "Weekend warriors: prepare for battle." The copywriter then tells readers, "It's Mother Nature versus you." The ad displays an amazing arsenal of power tools that average homeowners, "garden-variety gladiators," must have to overpower their landscapes: a power riding mower, an electric weed-whacker, even a chainsaw! The ad ends on a stirring note: "Show your yard that this is one turf war you plan on winning." You can almost hear martial drums beating in the background as you read this ad, yet most Americans see nothing amiss.

We are so far out of the environmental loop that we no longer realize that in nature, plants thrive on their own, without benefit of neighborhood garden centers. Plants that are indigenous to their area have "learned" over the millennia to exist and thrive in the local conditions. Natural landscapes are healthy habitats for wildlife; they coexist in harmony.

The typical American landscape, on the other hand, is populated by exotic species that are all too often ill suited to their new surroundings; many of them are invasive and upset the local ecology. The ground, which has been scraped and leveled by the builders, becomes host to every noxious weed in the vicinity; they love disturbed areas. Then topsoil is brought in, carrying another invasion of weeds. No wonder homeowners believe they need an arsenal from power implements to chemicals to maintain their properties. Having done everything wrong, they've guaranteed that their weekends will be plagued by landscape maintenance forever.

These *un*natural landscapes need artificial life support systems to exist. Go away for a month or two and you won't have a landscape when you return. Yet we are so divorced from nature that we think this is acceptable.

A natural landscape, on the other hand, filled with native flora, is largely self-sufficient and can exist on rainfall alone. This ecosystem is not a collection of individual plants, it is a community in which everything—including the wildlife—thrives in a harmonious and synergistic relationship.

WAKING UP

Happily, there is a growing awareness of our environment and a burgeoning respect for nature. And it's based on more than aesthetic appreciation. It is based on a new understanding of this interconnectedness and a realization that we cannot continue living in the wasteful manner to which we've become accustomed. Recycling is now commonplace. We strive to be more fuel efficient in business and in our daily lives. Rivers and lakes that were once little better than cesspools are being cleaned up and are once again full of fish and wading kids.

But this can still be likened to a slow awakening; environmentalism is still far from being a majority position, and it continues to rank low on the list of voter concerns in poll after poll, election after election. Given a choice between watching a *National Geographic* special or the umpteenth rerun of *Gilligan's Island*, guess which program most folks will tune in to.

PUTTING THE LAND FIRST

The purpose of this book is not to go into great detail on the threatened state of our world ecology. Many voices, far more articulate and persuasive than mine, are doing that already—and will continue to do so. The aim of this book is simply to introduce you to a relatively new and exciting technique for salvaging one small part of our environment: the natural land on which you will build a new home. Or office. Or shopping center.

This technique is very different from the traditional way we've been building because it respects nature. It puts the land first and preserves as much of the natural habitat as possible.

This new technique is most commonly called the "envelope." And, as we'll see in the following chapters, it is simple to execute, cost-effective, and very marketable, so the pragmatic bottom liners have no excuse for ignoring it.

I should point out that I did not invent the envelope approach to building; numerous people—architects, builders, and some homeowners—were using it long before I even became aware of it. In fact, the envelope was "invented" many times and in many parts of the country by people who were unaware that others shared their vision.

The envelope is not used identically in every case; different circumstances—terrain, home styles, personal tastes, etc.—result in a variety of executions. I found envelope homes in remote regions as well as on suburban lots that had escaped a builder's notice. The one element that unites them all is that they are built by people who care about the environment and want to minimize their impact on it. And that's the real bottom line: the envelope technique saves habitats. Put another way—it works with Mother Nature and not against her.

Years ago, when I was working in the ad business in New York, I was invited to join a lunch group that had formed among some of my coworkers. Once a week we would all go to a nice restaurant and, by pooling our money, purchase an expensive bottle of wine that we could not have afforded individually. In this way, I came to appreciate fine wine—an affliction that persists to this day. The point is, I would probably not have appreciated these fine vintages to the extent that I do had I not lifted so many glasses of cheap jug wine in the previous years. I had a context within which to truly understand what I was discovering.

We often do not grasp the importance of something new unless we have some familiarity with what preceded it. To fully appreciate the significance of nature's envelope, we'll take a look at three kinds of landscapes: two of them you create and one you preserve. Although the preserved landscape is the focus of this book, understanding the two created landscapes will help us view the preserved one in the proper perspective.

CREATED LANDSCAPES

The first created landscape is the one we are most familiar with. It's the one you grew up with and very likely have around your home right now. It is the traditional

A conventional high-maintenance, lawn-centered landscape. It requires ongoing care and feeding. watering, spraying, mowing, edging, raking, bagging, and pruning. In exchange for all this work, we get a clone of virtually all other landscapes in this country. Can you guess where this home is? East coast? West coast? Midwest? Canada?

lawn-centered landscape, with box hedges planted down the sidewalk or along the foundation and beds of exotic annuals or perennials, exotics being plants that are not native to where you live. They can be from halfway around the world, or from another and very different part of your own state. This landscape may have been designed and installed by the homeowners or they may have inherited it when they purchased the house. This kind of landscape is high maintenance and requires on-going care: watering, mowing, edging, spraying, weeding, bagging ... you name it.

The second created landscape is the one that uses plants that are native, or in-digenous, to the locale in which they are being used. These "natives" have adapted over the millennia to the soil conditions, the temperatures, and the rainfall of that region. They are genetically encoded with all the information they need to exist in those conditions. In addition, they have, over time, developed a harmonious and synergistic relationship to their habitat—both plants and animals.

DEFINING A NATIVE

Notice that when I talk about native plants, I refer to regions and not states. Even though it's done all the time, it isn't really accurate to refer to a plant as being na-tive to a specific state. Plants don't care about state lines; these are artificial political boundaries and have nothing to do with where the plant can thrive. In fact, all plants—except for some like tea roses that have been so highly selected and hy-bridized that they cannot exist in the wild—can be called natives; the question is, native to where?

Plants are native to vegetational regions, sometimes skipping large stretches of terrain and showing up again many hundreds of miles away. For example, the American smoke tree, *Cotinus obovatus*, is native to limestone canyons and hillsides in central Texas, the Ozarks, and the place where Alabama, Georgia, and Tennessee come together. These isolated populations may be separated by as much as 500 miles. Undoubtedly, these populations were once continuous, when the climate was different. Interestingly, all the relicts are on limestone with wind protection and a fair amount of sun. Companion plants at all locations are similar, including white ash (or the closely related Texas ash) and some form of blackhaw viburnum, an ornamental tree with bluish-purple fruits (haws) that are very popular with birds. But are the Tennessee trees more cold hardy? Are the Texas trees more drought tolerant? As the gene pools of plants are separated or are exposed to different climatic conditions, they start adjusting to those conditions. How much they differ depends on how many centuries they have been separated.

Even when the populations are continuous, the genetic makeup will differ if there are great differences in soil or climate. Big bluestem or old turkeyfoot *Andropogon gerardii* is the dominant grass of the tallgrass prairies, which in the 1850s stretched from Canada to central Texas. There is now a lot of interest in prairie restoration, so the federal government has a program that helps farmers revegetate old, worn-out farm fields with big bluestem and its three main companion grasses, little bluestem, Indiangrass, and switchgrass. The seed was all grown from one vigorous midwestern gene pool and was distributed throughout the tallgrass regions. But it

American smoketree Cotinus obovatus

Left: *Little bluestem* Schizachyrium scoparium *is a basic component of tallgrass, midgrass, and shortgrass prairies, and it is prized for its blue-green hues.* Center: *Indiangrass* Sorghastrum nutans *is spectacular when backlit by the sun, especially in the fall, when it is bright gold.* Right: *Switchgrass* Panicum virgatum *can be 8 feet tall and is native from Canada into Mexico.*

Joshua tree Yucca brevilolia *is the signature plant of the Mojave Desert. Inexplicably, Las Vegas homeowners rarely use it their landscapes, where it makes sense. Instead, they seem to favor the saguaro cactus, which does not! Moreover, thousands of Joshua trees are lost each year as they are bulldozed by developers.*

soon became abundantly clear that the federally distributed big bluestem was from a cold-hardy gene pool that was unable to survive a Texas summer.

There is another category of native plants: those that are native to one site only and are found nowhere else in the world. They are called *endemics*. One example is the Joshua tree, which is found only in the Mojave Desert that surrounds Las Vegas, Nevada. Another is the famous Texas bluebonnet, which is endemic to the limestone center of the Lone Star State.

The gardener who uses native plants instead of standard exotic nursery stock has an easier time of it. Watering is minimal because the native plants are xeriscapic. Gardeners like to add supplemental watering during especially dry periods or to simply keep the flora looking their photogenic best.

THE VERSATILITY OF NATIVES

A common misunderstanding about native landscapes is that they all look alike— "wild" and "unkempt." I've read articles by so-called gardening authorities who have said as much. One writer stated that the only way to be successful with native plants was "to live like a bear in the wilderness." This is, of course, total nonsense and reflects the writer's biases more than any actual experience with natives.

In fact, a native landscape is very versatile. In a book we wrote some years back, my wife, Sally, designed a very formal garden with parterres and topiary—just to prove that any style garden can be created using only native plants. This garden was symmetrical and would not have looked out of place in front of an old English manor house.

People who want the benefits of native plants but aren't ready to challenge the stylistic prejudices of their neighbors can achieve a very conventional look with native trees, shrubs, annuals, and perennials. Their native landscape can even have a native lawn. In the central United States, new varieties of buffalograss—Prairie and 609—are becoming very popular. Buffalograss requires minimal watering and, being very slow growing, only one or two mowings a season. Some people even allow it to reach its full height of six to eight inches and never mow at all.

A native landscape can also be very informal, mimicking Mother Nature in a more relaxed layout. Trees and shrubs get minimal pruning and are never shaped into "mushrooms" or "lollipops," as they are in many conventional landscapes. Certain well-adapted nonnatives can even be used. This style is called *naturalistic*, and it is gaining in popularity all over the country.

THE PRESERVED LANDSCAPE

The third kind of landscape is the one that nature's envelope is all about. It is the preserved landscape, and it is the easiest kind to have. It is established and mature and needs very little help from people. This is a difficult concept for many people to grasp. We were raised on the belief that plants need ongoing attention. They must be watered regularly and cared for, and it seems heretical to suggest that we just aren't needed.

And yet, ask yourself this question: How did those plants manage to survive all those many thousands of years before we showed up? They thrived long before there were garden centers, weekend gardening experts on the radio, and gardening magazines and books. The truth is, we kill as many plants by overwatering them as we do through neglect.

The preserved landscape may be virgin land, as yet untouched by our heavy hands, or it can be restored land, for example, a forest that had been farmland a half century before and has since revegetated itself with the assistance of wind-borne or animal-borne seeds. It is worth preserving in as intact a state as possible for many reasons: it requires minimal upkeep, it costs you virtually nothing, and it provides badly needed habitat for numerous species of wildlife that are declining in numbers because they are losing their feeding and nesting sites. Plus, of course, it's very attractive.

THE BIRTH OF THE CONVENTIONAL LANDSCAPE

People who have preserved, natural landscapes around their homes tend to be very enthusiastic about them and become more so the longer they live in this kind of environment. But for most people, this is a radical idea and a great departure from what we are used to. Having grown up with the traditional lawn-centered landscape, some people may find it difficult—even impossible—to entertain the notion of one that is less structured and controlled.

But, why are we so connected to this style? Why do we so easily (some might even say submissively) accept the idea that we must spend our weekends caring for their every need? As gardening author Ken Druse says in his book *The Natural Garden*, "I shudder when I think of the hours spent in mowing grass lawns, deadheading annuals, shearing hedges, feeding, spraying, and so on. In this cycle of perpetual care, you quickly become a slave to your environment rather than a participant in its beautification."

How then did we get stuck with the lawn-centered landscape?

Believe it or not, serious consideration has been given to the idea that our affinity for lawns is *genetic*. In other words, we can't help it. Biologist John Falk contends that our prehistoric ancestors in the savannas of Africa found short grass a definite asset in the survival game; it allowed them to spot predators at a distance. Falk calls this "adapted predisposition" and admits that evidence is circumstantial at best, but the thesis is not unreasonable. Given countless generations of this kind of thinking, it becomes clear why we feel safe and secure with short grass around us.

Cultivated lawns have been with us for many centuries. Cultures throughout history, from Europe to the Far East, have maintained lawns as centerpieces of their domestic and public areas. But it was in eighteenth-century England, through the efforts of eminent landscapers such as William Kent and Lancelot "Capability" Brown, that the lawn achieved its full prominence. Brown, especially, had a passion for vast stretches of grass, and he uprooted large gardens, displaced villages, and chopped down great stands of trees to make room for his planes of grass. Scottish landscaper Ian Hamilton Finlay said that Brown "makes water appear as Water and lawn as Lawn."

Lawns surrounded all the great houses in England and became a mark of distinction and even ostentatious display. This was not lost on the common folk, who viewed lawns as symbols of "having made it." Years later, when millions of immigrants found their way to the New World, little wonder that as soon as they could manage it, they had lawns around their own homes.

BLAME IT ON FRANK

Our present dependence on the manicured, lawn-centered landscape can be laid at the feet of one man: Frank J. Scott (no relation to the seed company). In the latter half of the nineteenth century, suburbia was being born. It was a far cry from the suburban boom that followed World War II, but it was suburbia nonetheless. Until that time, people either lived a rural existence or they lived in cities in townhomes or apartments. For the city dwellers, the urge to have more elbow room and fresher air dictated a move, usually of no more than a few blocks from the heart of downtown.

Here, streets were lined with brand-new homes and empty yards. Trouble was, those novice suburbanites had no idea what to do with those yards. The urbanites had never had yards to worry about while the country folk on farms had had experience with dirt front yards that merely required periodic sweeping.

Enter Frank Scott, a successful landscape architect in Cincinnati. In 1870, Scott published a book designed to help these fledgling suburbanites cope with this new situation. It was called *The Art of Beautifying Suburban Home Grounds*, and it was an instant best-seller. In it, Scott told homeowners that "a smooth, closely shaven surface of grass is by far the most essential element of beauty on the grounds of a suburban home."

About the same time, the first U.S. patent was issued for the lawn mower, followed closely by a patent on a lawn sprinkler. By the early part of the twentieth century, the suburban home and lawn were a fixture of American life, and homeowners—usually men—were spending more of their time caring for it. They were also spending more time on golf courses, and from that an interesting synergy resulted.

Golfers, impressed by the condition of the courses they played on, turned to the club greens keepers for help in making their home lawns more picture perfect. Before long, golf pros such as Sammy Snead and Bobby Jones—and later Jack Nicklaus and Arnold Palmer—appeared in ads endorsing lawn-care products.

Suburbia really took off after World War II, when developers such as William Levitt began producing homes with assembly line efficiency to meet the demands of millions of discharged servicemen and women looking for the American Dream. These new homes, of course, had to have lawns, along with the proverbial picket fences and rose arbors. Wartime production of munitions and chemicals was rapidly converted to fertilizers and pesticides and herbicides, and ads in magazines touted the "perfect lawn."

One ad asks, "Got Garden Pests?" and shows a voracious beetle chopping away on the leaves of a shrub—every gardener's nightmare! Not to worry, the ad assures the reader. The solution is something called End-O-Pest, which promises to rid the garden of "chewing insects, sucking insects, and fungus diseases." The reader is led to believe that all insects are the enemy, for the garden must be perfect. Another ad celebrates the "picture-book beauty" of the ideal lawn, and it's "so easy with Vertagreen." The Hudson Company promotes its sprayers and dusters for applying chemicals to control pests and weeds. And, they enthuse, "Ladies, you'll love this finest, lightest 1 ¾ gallon sprayer." An ad from the folks at American Chemical Paint Company shows a beaming six-year-old girl with a wheelbarrow full of blossoms that grew happily in the weed-free garden because her parents—also beaming—were smart enough to use Weedone. One wonders if the grass beneath her feet is still damp from the toxic spray.

Anyone looking at these ads today, in our more environmentally aware age, has to notice that these products were all petroleum based; there was nothing natural about them, and we were laying the groundwork for millions of health problems, ranging from skin rashes to cancer, resulting from these toxic chemicals.

WEEDS OR WILDFLOWERS?

We were also conforming to the approved look set down by Frank J. Scott many years before. There were always some who would have nothing to do with this overly controlled, disciplined approach to landscaping, but they were (and still are) a minority. In fact, Peter Henderson, a contemporary of Scott's, wrote in his own book *Gardening for Pleasure*, exactly what he thought about these renegades: "It is gratifying to know that such neighbors are not numerous, for the example of the majority will soon shame them into decency." Incredibly, having the "right" kind of landscape had become a moral issue, and we were facing what might be called, "the tyranny of the neighbors."

This tyranny is best exemplified by the misuse of municipal weed ordinances. Weed laws were first enacted in the early part of the twentieth century and were designed to benefit the agriculture industry by regulating specific plants—noxious weeds—that were harmful to farm crops. These included crabgrass, chickweed, johnsongrass, bindweed, and a variety of thistles. These laws were necessary and beneficial, and they were usually enacted at the state level. Today, agricultural

Just three of the many noxious weed grasses plaguing homeowners, prairie restorationists, and farmers. From left to right: quack grass, Hungarian brome, and canary reed grass.

weed laws are still required because farmers are still plagued by these weeds and other invasives from foreign shores—Russian knapweed, Hungarian brome, quack grass, canary reed grass, Canada thistle, leafy spurge, and yellow toadflax, to name a few.

Because these weeds are so invasive, they soon began showing up in suburban neighborhoods, and then counties, municipalities, and even subdivision property owner associations began enacting their own weed laws and covenants. Often these strictures outlawed, not specific noxious species, but any unfamiliar herbacious vegetation that grew over some arbitrary height imposed by community standards.

Community weed laws are not bad of themselves. They protect property owners from uncaring neighbors who allow their own property to become overgrown and trashy. Nobody wants this. The problem arises when no differentiation is made between unkempt yards filled with noxious weeds and yards full of healthy native vegetation. Plants get labeled as weeds simply because they are unknown to the neighbors. They are not common nursery stock and are therefore suspect and even condemned. The old adage can be reversed: "Unfamiliarity breeds contempt."

Ralph Waldo Emerson declared that "a weed is a wildflower that hasn't been appreciated yet." Others say that "wildflower" is simply a euphemism for "weed." Too simplistic? Many think so, and they identify weeds as plants that do not belong where they are found and can be harmful to the environment, such as invasives. Wildflowers and other native vegetation most certainly belong where they are found because they have been there far longer then we have.

A major part of the problem has to do with the simple fact that we are a conforming species, and we view with alarm and distaste anyone who dares to deviate from the norm, in this case, the conventionally manicured yard. Homeowners who adopt a more relaxed style of landscaping, mimicking Mother Nature with indigenous plants in a naturalistic style, may find themselves the recipients of citations from their community—not praising their efforts but demanding they cut down the offending vegetation and fall in line or risk stiff fines.

It happens all over the country. In 1986, Nancy and Walter Stewart converted their Maryland property into a natural meadow filled with wildflowers and native meadow grasses. The neighbors saw weeds and called the Stewarts' landscape a "disgrace." The county cited the couple, but when Nancy, an attorney, threatened a legal challenge, the county backed down.

Ned Fritz, a Dallas attorney and author, had to go to court to defend his right to grow sunflowers, goldenrod, and Virginia wild rye in his front yard. He brought in expert witnesses who demonstrated that his vegetation did not meet the city's definition of weeds as "unwanted plants."

Time and again, challenges to natural landscaping are defeated for the simple reason that all the supposed dangers and threats to health and welfare put forth are shown to be without scientific foundation. Opponents say natural landscapes attract vermin. Yet vermin, such as Norway rats, live in garbage; there is nothing in a healthy natural landscape to attract or sustain them. Opponents say natural landscapes are fire hazards, yet any landscape can burn. If a home catches fire, neighboring trees and roofs also ignite whether the rest of the landscape is lawn or forest or chaparral. Homeowners with prairie landscapes burn them on purpose, but the dry grasses burn too fast to pose any real danger. Moreover, periodic burns are a long-standing and proven means of maintaining the health and beauty of such a landscape.

Bret Rappaport, a Chicago attorney who has successfully fought numerous such cases, has authored a booklet on weed laws that is available through the John Marshall Law School in Chicago. In it he details the history of weed laws and suggests numerous ways to combat and change unfair weed laws. Through his work, he has become a vocal advocate for natural landscapes. "If we can grant our neighbors the right to have shaved lawns and colored gravel, tacky concrete statuary and astroturf on the front porch," he asks, "why then can't we also grant people the right to have environmentally sound and beneficial natural landscapes?"

THE TREND TOWARD NATURAL

In fact, we are. More and more, natural landscapes are becoming a common sight in neighborhoods all over America. A homeowner in a Milwaukee suburb, Rochelle Whiteman, discovered that she did not have to defend her natural landscape. Rather, she had to share it with neighbors who came to her and asked for help in establishing their own prairie and woodland gardens.

And the trend will continue. David Northington, former executive director of the Lady Bird Johnson Wildflower Center (formerly the National Wildflower Research Center) in Austin, Texas, has predicted that the natural landscape will, by the second or third decade of the twenty-first century, be not only commonplace

Once, Rochelle and Paul Whiteman had the only prairie landscape in their suburban Milwaukee neighborhood. Instead of being prosecuted by the city, Rochelle became the local native plant guru and has helped a number of her neighbors install and maintain natural landscapes of their own.

but the rule. His belief is based on the fact that water will become more and more precious in the decades ahead, and people will have to seek more drought-tolerant means of landscaping their homes. "The conventional lawn-centered landscape of today, " he says, "will one day be viewed as an example of our wasteful past."

And if you think he is being overly optimistic, consider that in only a few decades we have gone from a society that accepted smoking virtually anywhere and at anytime to one in which nonsmoking office buildings, airplanes, hotel rooms, and restaurants are commonplace.

The Importance of Habitats 3

It was the midpoint between the end of the Revolutionary War and the Louisiana Purchase. We had beaten the mighty British Empire and won our independence, and we were feeling more than a little cocky. In 1792, General Benjamin Lincoln expressed the muscle-flexing expansionist sentiments of his fellow Americans when he stated, "Civilization directs us to remove as fast as possible that natural growth from the lands." Interestingly, his words reflect not just the attitude of his day but the attitude of many of our contemporaries.

If you are over thirty and you happen to revisit a remote natural area you haven't seen since you were a kid, odds are that you'll find it significantly changed. If a housing development hasn't appeared on the scene, then at the very least you'll find that the quaint dirt road has been paved and lined with telephone poles. Where the mom-and-pop gas station and bait shop once stood in the shade of venerable oak trees there is now a slick strip mall that includes a convenience store selling lottery tickets and frozen drink concoctions, a marine supplies dealer, and a real estate office.

It wouldn't hurt us to look at Europe and recall the great forests that once covered that continent. They were felled to create farmland, to harvest lumber for new homes, and to make charcoal for the early stages of the Industrial Revolution.

Where they were felled in dry habitats, such as the oak forests in Spain that were cut down to build the Spanish Armada, they never grew back. Sherwood Forest, once a dense woodland that was the legendary home of Robin Hood and his merry men, is now suburbia. Germany's famous Black Forest is dying because of air pollution.

Today, forests are disappearing in South and Central America, and all over Asia, to meet the needs of their soaring populations. Amazon rain forests are cut down to create farmland, but when these forests disappear, ironically so does the rainfall that would make the farms viable. These forests, like all living entities, transpire, and the moisture that rises up from this dense habitat comes down again as rain— as much as nine feet of it a year!

Forests are disappearing here, as well. This is cause for more than passing concern because our forests play a vital role in maintaining the environmental health of the entire planet. Forests produce oxygen, absorb carbon dioxide from the atmosphere, and stabilize the climate. Clearly, wanton destruction of this resource is nothing less than mindless suicide.

But it isn't only woodlands that are vanishing. Less than 0.5 percent of our original prairies are still intact, while deserts, wetlands, and savannas are seriously threatened. These are also habitats for countless species of animal life, many of which have yet to be discovered and catalogued. When broadcaster Michael Reagan tells his listeners that "environmentalists care more about squirrels than they do about people," any listener with even a smattering of knowledge about natural science should understand how preposterous that statement is. It is not an either/or situation. People and squirrels—not to mention spotted owls, snow leopards, humpback whales, bats, and countless endangered native flora—are all part and parcel of this marvelous and mysterious and interdependent whole we call life. The fate of one affects all the rest of us. In fact, we must live this way or we're all in a lot of trouble.

A few years ago, a TV commercial showed a young teacher leading her tiny charges on a field trip to the big city. As they come out of the subway, they all join hands to cross the busy street, and the voice-over says, "What's the first thing we need to know? If we're going to get somewhere, we have to get there together."

DECLINING WILDLIFE POPULATIONS

A few years back a woman approached me after one of my talks and remarked that she wasn't seeing as many songbirds as she had when she was a girl. Understand, she wasn't a senior citizen, she was in her middle forties. It wasn't the first time I'd heard that statement.

It made me recall when I was a kid growing up in suburban New Jersey, chasing around the yard with a jar capturing fireflies. They were plentiful, but so were Japanese beetles. We had only recently begun carrying out chemical warfare on garden "pests."

We have been conducting chemical warfare on our landscapes for the better part of a century. But garden pests, weeds, and fungi are not the only living things affected by these toxins. We have also managed to kill off an amazing number of friendly creatures while at the same time inflicting everything from skin rashes to cancer on ourselves.

Today, all those decades of spraying have resulted in major health problems for ourselves and a sharp decline, not just in garden pests, but in many other life forms as well, including native predator insects that help control the pests. Consider that only 1 percent of all the insects in a typical garden can be called pests. The other 99 percent are either benign or beneficial. And all that spraying doesn't just affect the insects. Toxic sprays kill birds and butterflies and other creatures as well—directly and indirectly. For example, by poisoning insects we eliminate an important protein source for nesting songbirds.

Herbicides too kill more than weeds. One recent and alarming example: We have created a new generation of genetically engineered corn and soybeans crops that are described as "Round-up ready." That means they can be "safely" sprayed with the popular herbicide to rid agricultural settings of milkweed. But did the inventors and promoters of this "scientific marvel" realize that milkweed is what monarch butterfly larvae feed upon? Chip Taylor, head of the Entomology

The Monarch butterfly Danaus plexippus *is threatened by our ability to create scientific marvels. By producing genetically altered crops that are "Round-up safe," we can now rid rows of corn and soybeans of milkweed ... which Monarchs feed upon.*

Department at the University of Kansas and director of Monarch Watch, says these new corn and soybean crops will "raise hell with monarchs." These new crops are being increasingly used from Nebraska to Pennsylvania, and the real possibility exists that our grandchildren will grow up never having seen one of these magnificent creatures.

We are an amazingly short-sighted species when it comes to living with nature. Too often we do things simply because we can, giving little or no thought to possible consequences. We imported grasses such as Hungarian brome, K R bluestem, and downy chess as cattle feed, and then we watched as they spread virtually unchecked across the land, invading and destroying native prairies. In 1890, someone imported sixty starlings just because they were pretty; today starlings are a major problem all over the country, aggressively outcompeting native birds and contributing to their decline.

And by overusing pesticides, we appear to be creating new breeds of "super-pests" that are resistant to these poisons, necessitating, of course, the use of even stronger toxins. And so on. Time and again we solve problems—real or perceived—by interfering with nature, only to create new problems. The blame, according to Vice President Al Gore, is our "focus on short-term exploitation at the expense of the long-term health of the system itself."

Extinction, of course, is not new. It creeps along at a slow and steady pace for eons and then bursts into vast exterminations that utterly change the world. One of the largest mass extinctions occurred 240 million years ago in the Permian seas (where west Texas is today). At that time, 95 percent of all animal species disappeared. Another spectacular extinction came at the end of the Cretaceous era 65 million years ago when dinosaurs, along with 70 percent of the other species known to exist at that time, died. A mini–mass extinction occurred in the Americas 11,000 years ago after the last ice age when approximately seventy species of elephants, camels, horses, and other large mammals disappeared, possibly with the help of Clovis man.

Midway into the twentieth century, botanists and biologists noticed that the rate of extinction was again escalating. We are now losing animal species a thousand times faster than we have been for the last 10,000 years. Not surprisingly, this seems to have coincided with our precipitous population explosion. *The more of us there are on the planet, the fewer there seem to be of every other life form.*

For as bad as toxins have been for wildlife, according to the Audubon Society and other organizations that track wildlife populations, the number one cause of their declining numbers has been loss of habitat. And that ties in directly to our own growing population. As we build more and more housing developments, shopping centers, business parks, as well as the vast network of roads and highways to connect them all, we are destroying wildlife nesting and feeding sites and disrupting migratory routes.

Deer, coyotes, foxes, and other mammals increasingly "invade" suburbia, not because they are intent on doing us harm but because they simply have nowhere else to go in their quest for food. Newsweek magazine noted that cougars had been spotted near shopping malls in Arizona, and a woman living in a suburban neighborhood in Colorado Springs told me that coyotes were seen near a local school. When I asked her if seeing wild animals in the area scared her, she responded, "Of course not. We enjoy it." And then she added, "After all, we moved into their neighborhood, they didn't move into ours."

In her book *The Once and Future Forest*, Leslie Sauer notes that "in our sprawling, developed landscapes, every patch of green has become an increasingly important remnant in an ever more tattered fabric."

ANATOMY OF A HABITAT

Preserving habitats is what this book is all about. But before we get into the "nuts and bolts" of nature's envelope, let's look at what it is we are preserving.

A basic mistake most people make with regard to landscaping is to think of plants as individuals. This no doubt explains why we see so many massed floral displays in public and private gardens. A hundred of more marigolds or begonias or tulips or hostas clumped together, often all of the same color, is considered by some to be a breathtakingly gorgeous sight, and the epitome of horticultural excellence. For this reason, many botanical gardens greet visitors by placing large beds of monochromatic exotics near the entrance, assuring that their tour will begin with lots of oohs and aahs.

But other visitors—admittedly still a minority—find such displays boring and find the complexity and interrelatedness of Mother Nature's landscapes far more

Plants should not be thought of as individuals but as members of communities. Southern lady fern coexists naturally with Carolina phlox and fire pink along the Blue Ridge Parkway in North Carolina. Contrast the color and texture of this scene with typical garden plantings that mass just one species and color.

interesting. In nature, plants do not really exist as individuals; they exist as part of communities. In a natural setting you can see forty or more species thriving within a relatively small area—trees, shrubs, vines, ground covers, wildflowers, grasses—all living in harmony.

The natural habitat is a self-sustaining environment, home not just to all these numerous companion plants but to many forms of wildlife—birds, insects, mammals—that are a necessary part of this incredible tapestry we call the natural world.

The components of a natural habitat will, of course, vary from region to region. For instance, tall canopy or shade trees are common along the eastern seaboard and in the Northwest, but in the prairie regions and the southwestern deserts, the only tall trees are often down along the rivers. To help you better understand the habitats of your own part of the country, let's take a brief look at the basic elements. In each general category, I've listed some of the plants within that category by their common names. The purpose here is not to provide a comprehensive and detailed profile of these plants but simply to give you some idea of the incredible and bountiful variety Mother Nature has provided.

Canopy Trees

Trees can be divided into tall trees, called canopy, and short trees, called ornamentals. Canopy trees, being the largest element in a habitat, usually give their name to that habitat. Towering over woodland settings from Canada down the East Coast to the Deep South and South through Washington, Oregon, Idaho, and Northern California, these arborial giants, when mature, rise from 50 feet to over 200 feet. Soil is a major factor in determining how tall a tree will grow, and in the southern states, where soils are often loose and deep and rainfall is ample all year, canopy trees can grow well over 100 feet, Even some understory trees can reach over 50 feet, southern magnolia being a good example.

Canopy trees are the linchpin without which the entire plant community would fall apart or would be dramatically altered. They are also extremely long-lived and can survive one to three centuries. Canopy trees are either deciduous, that is, they shed their leaves each fall, or they are evergreen, their leaves or needles stay green all year. The fallen leaves of deciduous canopy trees decompose and form rich new soil on the woodland floor, while their shade provides a comfortable environment for numerous understory plants, from ferns to woodland wildflowers.

The deciduous trees are perhaps most appreciated for their fabulous fall colors. Triggered by cold snaps, the leaves change color and display hues ranging from burgundies and reds to oranges and golden yellows and rusts.

Deciduous canopy trees include oaks, elms, beeches, hickories, maples, sweetgums, sycamores, ashes, lindens, pecans, hackberries, walnuts, and cottonwoods. Evergreen canopy trees are spruces, firs, Douglas fir, pines, live oaks, Montezuma cypress, or California fan palm.

Deciduous canopy trees such as this bigtooth maple Acer grandidentatum *are noted for their brilliant fall colors. Even blasé urban dwellers are tempted out into the countryside when autumn leaves turn.*

The tree that is dominant determines a specific habitat. For example, the size and number of California fan palms will control the character of an oasis in the southern Colorado Desert in California. Montezuma cypress, more prevalent in Mexico, mixes with Texas palm in Brownsville, Texas, near the Rio Grande River to form the lushest habitat of that region. Various species of live oaks can be found along the Gulf Coast, in southern California, and in the Texas Hill Country, but they all have a distinctive look with their broad crowns and dark, spreading arms. Firs and spruces, found in Alaska, Canada, and at high elevations, jam themselves together to make forests that are tall, dark, narrow, and superbly adapted to snow.

Frequently, two species, like fir and spruce, share domination of a habitat. Pines and oaks often join together, especially in poor, dry, or sandy soil, to make wildly different habitats such as the New Jersey pine barrens, the ponderosa savannas of the Rocky Mountains, or the longleaf pine savannas of the Deep South.

Some trees are adapted to a wide range of climate and may participate in more than one kind of habitat. For example, American beech shares dominance with sugar maples in Indiana to make beech-maple forest. But in Mississippi, it combines with southern magnolia to make beech-magnolia forest.

Ornamental Trees

Unlike canopy trees, ornamental trees have brightly colored flowers and juicy fruits that feed birds and mammals. These ornamental trees fall into two main cate-

Sometimes lanceleaf sumac
Rhus lanceolata *is a thirty-foot tall ornamental tree with only one trunk, but more frequently it is a thicket less than ten feet high. In summer, it has white pyramids of flowers that feed bees and butterflies. In early fall, red fruits feed migrating birds and can be used to make a lemonade-tasting drink.*

gories. Understory trees prefer the shade and highly organic soil they find under canopy trees. Other ornamentals thrive only in sunny habitats, such as deserts, or landscapes that are frequently burned, such as savannas.

Ornamental trees are usually ten to fifty feet high. The understory ornamentals tend to be one-third to one-half the height of the canopy trees they grow beneath. Often they are multitrunked, and there are endless, unresolvable debates about whether some of these beauties should be called small trees or large shrubs.

Native ornamentals tend to have more descriptive names than do the shade trees; some are fairly obvious, such as Eve's necklace, which displays dangling strings of beadlike fruits each fall. Some can even be humorous, like ape's earring. A sampling from around the country includes devil's walking stick, chokeberry, moosewood, orchid tree, pawpaw, musclewood, saskatoon, fringe tree, fiddlewood, roughleaf dogwood, American smoke tree, sandpaper tree, kidneywood, two-winged silverbell, witch hazel, possumhaw, goldenball leadtree, Jerusalem thorn, staggerbush, and horsesugar.

Shrubs

Smaller than ornamental trees, some shrubs grow tall enough to cause confusion even among experts. In the South, rosebay rhododendron is classified as a shrub even though it can, on rare occasions, reach forty feet. Texas mountain laurel is often classified as a shrub; being slow growing, it stays under six feet for many years, and it is seen growing in thickets. It is also multistemmed. Sounds like a

The itea Itea virginica, *also called Virginia willow and Virginia sweetspire, is found in moist to wet areas throughout the eastern United States (zones 6–9). This shrub provides erosion control along streams and is happiest in moderate to full shade.*

shrub. But it can be thirty feet tall, its stems make large trunks, and you can walk under it. Sounds like a tree.

Then there are shrubs so short—some less than six inches high—that most people think of them as flowers or ground covers. But they are classified as shrubs because they have woody stems, are shorter than a tree, are not obviously vines, and do not die back to the ground each year like flowers and grasses. A great many of these minatures are warm desert flowers that live a long time and never go dormant, so that the stems become woody.

Many shrubs are thicket forming. This enables them to move to a better location without having to start all over again from seed. Flameleaf sumac, for example, likes sun. If it comes up in a sunny meadow but later becomes overshadowed by trees, it can move back out into the sun by sending up new shoots from underground rhizomes. Some shrubs can spread several feet a year in this way and, unless they get pruned back periodically, can be pests.

Often desert succulents, such as cacti, yuccas, and agaves, are put in the shrub category, as they are permanent, shorter-than-tree members of the landscape.

The Ground Layer

In a conventional landscape, the ground layer is called ground cover or lawn. But in nature, it constitutes a far more flexible idea and exists to stop erosion, absorb and hold moisture, and build up more topsoil. The ground layer might be prairie, meadow, low thickets, ferns, woodland flowers, vines, lichens, mosses, decomposing leaves, or a crust of soil and rocks called "desert pavement."

Topsoil itself is a garden in microcosm. It contains soil bacteria and soil fungi that help a plant's roots absorb water and nutrients. It contains the "seed bank," in

The cabins at Thirty Mile Camp near Creede, Colorado, are surrounded by native ground layer plants that seeded in on their own. Under the aspen are meadowrue, ferns, and shade-loving flowers. In the sunny area around the cabin are grasses and sun-loving flowers such as penstemons and potentillas.

which seeds can be stored for decades until they are needed again. Some seeds can lie dormant for a hundred years or more awaiting an event such as an earthquake or a buffalo stampede. If a shady, centuries-old forest is destroyed by fire, flood, or wind, sun-loving seeds are in the soil ready to start the process of revegetation. As shade again develops, the already present seeds of shade-loving species begin to germinate to replace the sunny species that are dying out. This is called "succession." *When the topsoil is removed by bulldozer or erosion, future generations of native plants disappear along with its history, and the land is vulnerable to weeds.*

Invasive weeds are plants that prevent the natural process of succession from taking place. They are not a natural part of native habitats. Most weeds come from other continents. Although some are noninvasive, the ones that are cannot live harmoniously within our native habitats and do great environmental harm. These weeds, just like native pioneer plants, come into recently destroyed sites and prevent erosion. But then they do not let the more permanent plants take over to develop a rich and complex habitat. A few species greedily hold the site in perpetual adolescence. Instead of dozens of species, there are four or five. Usually weeds are annuals or biennials, but some are perennials. Some perennial weeds can invade a centuries-old habitat, replacing hundreds of native species with just one.

Because there are now more weed seeds than native seeds in the air and water, fighting weeds is a necessary part of maintaining a native habitat. It is comforting,

Purple loosestrife Lythrum salicaria *is a highly invasive perennial "weed" that is native to Eurasia. It came to the United States in the early 1800s and has since spread throughout the temperate zones of North America, colonizing wetlands, meadows, marshes, and the shorelines of lakes and rivers. New England experienced a particularly bad outbreak in 1998–99. Purple loosestrife outcompetes native species, threatens rare and endangered natives, and reduces available food and shelter for wildlife. Like many invasives, it is attractive, so it is difficult to convince people that it is a serious environmental threat. Although many nurseries still sell purple loosestrife, one nursery owner told me that he refuses—even though he gets requests for it.*

however, that there are fewer weeds in an established habitat. *Keeping the ground layer undisturbed is the best protection against weeds.*

EXAMPLES OF SPECIFIC HABITATS

Trees, shrubs, and the ground layer are the three basic components of any habitat you might choose to live in. But the height, density, and number of species can vary considerably. Here are sketches of some very different habitats to give you a better idea of what a habitat landscape is.

You may notice that prairies are left out. That is because your chances of finding a prairie to preserve are minuscule. The creek woodlands in the prairie states are also heavily degraded. Those near the home that we had in Dallas, Texas, might be termed "Asian-Texas woodlands," as the understory is almost entirely from China or Japan; only the canopy trees are native. To have your house surrounded by prairie, bur oak savanna, elm-ash riparian woodland, or other midwestern habitats, you would need to do a restoration. If you can find remnants of such habitats near you, then it should be possible to follow the guidelines in chapter 6, "Revegetation," to help you plant a native habitat from scratch.

Coniferous Forest

Coniferous forests are composed mainly of conifers, which include spruce, fir, pine, juniper, sequoia, and hemlock. These forests successfully cope with little available water because of frozen soil, deep sand, or steep slopes. Most of Canada, the Pacific Northwest, and mountaintops below the tundra or tree line are covered with coniferous forest. In Maine, a coniferous forest might consist mainly of hem-

Three kinds of coniferous forest are visible in this picture of Taos Mountain in northern New Mexico. The dark green trees on the top third of the mountain are primarily spruce and fir. They are interrupted by rocky slopes too steep for trees. The brighter greens below are dominated by Douglas fir with aspens in the crevices. The yellow greens on the lower, flatter foothills are piñon-juniper scrub. Every once in a while, a taller, lighter green pine with longer needles rises up out of the scrub. These are ponderosas.

This view of a spruce-aspen habitat at the Taos Ski Valley shows an understory of Rocky Mountain maple, fireweed, wild geranium, thimble-berry, and souring rush, plus a host of other herbs, grasses, sedges, mosses, and mushroom.

lock and white pine. In the Appalachians, it is likely to be dominated by Fraser fir, red spruce, yellow birch, and rhododendron. In Estes Park, Colorado, building sites would typically include Douglas fir and aspen or ponderosa pine. In the central Sierra Nevadas of California, you might build in a forest of ponderosa pine, sugar pine, and giant sequoia. One coniferous habitat that is seeing a lot of construction is the western hemlock–Douglas fir forests in the Pacific Northwest. We'll look at that in more detail, as well as at the very different-looking spruce-fir forest in the Catskills.

Western Hemlock–Douglas Fir Forest in the Pacific Northwest

This type of forest can be found from sea level up to 3,000 feet in the Coast Ranges, Olympic Mountains, and the Cascade Range. Because temperatures are mild, there are many evergreens, and the forest is tall. Douglas firs are usually around 120 feet high and may get twice that, whereas western hemlocks may attain 225 feet.

Major trees are western hemlock, Douglas fir, and western red cedar. Minor trees are Sitka spruce, coast redwood, grand fir, and western white pine on the coast; inland there might be sugar pine, incense cedar, and ponderosa pine. Pacific silver fir is found at high elevations.

Smaller ornamental trees might be western yew, red alder, bigleaf maple, bitter cherry, Pacific madrone, golden chinkapin, and Garry oak.

Shrubs are likely to be Cascade Oregon grape and Pacific rhododendron, with salal, oceanspray *Holodiscus discolor*, and mountain balm *Ceanothus velutinus* at the dry end of the spectrum and vine maple at the moist.

Ground layer plants at the moist gradient might be sword fern and pink-flowered *Oxalis oregana*, possibly with thimbleberry or salmonberry. Drier areas will probably have that low shrubby ground cover kinnikinnik. Common herbaceous flowers capable of making a good show are vanilla leaf, which makes a beautiful, shin-high carpet of fragrant leaves, a yellow-flowered evergreen violet *Viola sempervirens*, the large, white-flowered wake robin *Trillium ovatum*, twinflower, inside-out flower, starflower, and bedstraw. The flowers are generally whites or pastels, as these colors show up best in a shady setting.

Where the soil has been disturbed, pioneer flowers are woodland groundsel *Senecio sylvaticus* and fireweed. The two together make a beautiful Band-Aid of bright yellow and hot pink the second summer. By the fifth year, shrubs begin to outnumber the herbaceous perennials.

Spruce–Fir Forest in the Catskills

Eastern spruce-fir forests occur above 4,500 feet in the Great Smoky Mountains, above 3,700 feet in the high plateaus of the Catskill Mountains in New York, above 2,200 feet in the Green Mountains of Vermont and the White Mountains of New Hampshire, and above 450 feet in Maine. The plant palette in all these locations is fairly consistent.

This is an evergreen forest with numerous tall, straight trunks and a ferny-

mossy ground layer that is about knee-high or lower. The middle layer of ornamental trees and shrubs is scant compared to the other forest habitats described
here. The soil is moist and acid.

In the Catskills, the main trees are balsam fir and red spruce. There are more
balsam firs, but the red spruces are taller (90 feet) and older (200–250 years), and
they have larger trunks. Other prominent trees are yellow birch, mountain paper
birch, moosewood (striped maple), American mountain ash, mountain maple, serviceberry, pin cherry, red maple, American beech, and eastern hemlock.

Tall shrubs are rosebay rhododendron, which is evergreen, and deciduous
shrubs such as rosebud azalea, and a couple of species of viburnum such as squash-
berry or hobblebush.

Smaller shrubs are likely to be huckleberries.

Ferns of various kinds are common in the ground layer: even shorter than the
ferns are northern wood sorrel and numerous species of mosses.

Shrublands, Savannas, and Woodlands

Shrublands, more commonly called chaparral, are a dense, short woody habitat—a
giant thicket. The foothills above Los Angeles are covered with chaparral. So are
the slopes of Mount Lemmon north of Tucson. Scrub oak-mountain mahogany
shrubland occurs in southern Wyoming and northern Utah beween the coniferous
forests and the desert.

In savannas, trees and shrubs cover a third of the area, and the other two thirds is
covered by grasses and flowers. Because savannas are fire dependent, and fires have
been suppressed for 150 to 300 years, savannas have mostly turned into woodlands.

Woodlands are denser than savannas, but there is still no continuous canopy, allowing plenty of sunlight to fall on the ground layer. Arlington, Texas, used to be
covered in post oak savanna, and the savanna has thickened into many acres of post
oak woodland currently being sold as residential lots. Oak woodlands make beautiful building sites because they are open and easy to walk in, and they offer a pleasing mixture of shade and sun.

The Portola Valley Ranch (profiled in chapter 8) is set in blue oak woodland. The
famous Hill Country in central Texas is dominated by juniper woodland. The sandhills in the Carolinas are longleaf pine savanna, a habitat that extends across the
South from the Atlantic to East Texas, wherever sands are deep and winters are mild.

Blue Oak Woodland in Central California

Blue oak woodland rings the Central Valley of California at elevations from 300
feet to 3,600 feet. The blue oaks range from fourteen to forty-five feet in height,
and their crowns do not meet. As a result, this woodland has sunny spots with
clumps of grasses and brightly colored wildflowers.

The major tree here is blue oak. Companion trees, varying according to site, are
coast live oak, interior live oak, digger pine, valley oak, or Kellogg's black oak.

The most ubiquitous ornamental tree is California buckeye.

Tall shrubs, head high, are scattered, so there is plenty of room for paths and private seating areas. These shrubs often grow tall enough to be pruned as small trees. Common species are manzanitas, wild lilacs *Ceanothus*, western redbud, toyon, coffeeberries, and redberries.

The ground layer is likely to be mostly nonnative annual grasses and a mixture of native and nonnative flowers. You need to leave the existing ground layer intact to prevent erosion, adding seeds of native perennial grasses and flowers. If you mow only once a year in late summer, just before fall rains begin, the longer-lived natives will gradually increase and outnumber the nonnatives.

California native grasses are, for the most part, silvery green with a delicate texture. They grow knee-high. The highly desirable needlegrasses and oniongrass are green in fall and winter; they flower in the spring and are dry golden for the rainless summers.

Native wildflowers in California are fairly spectacular in numbers and diversity. Your local chapter of the California Native Plant Society (see appendix) should be able to advise you on the best species, sources, and methods for planting and maintaining flowery grasslands.

Hill Country Juniper near Austin, Texas

The home of the golden-cheeked warbler is beautiful country all year round. The Ashe junipers, locally called mountain cedar, are fifteen to thirty-five feet tall. Where the junipers predominate, the habitat is known as "cedar brakes." As in the blue oak woodlands of California, there are lots of hot, sunny spaces between the junipers for flowers and grasses. On hilltops, there are often big bald spots of exposed limestone rock. The basic colors here are green juniper, golden grasses, and white rock.

The most ubiquitous and long-lived tree is the Ashe juniper, which some botanists classify as a large shrub. The shaggy-barked limbs branch out close to the ground, giving Ashe juniper a very short main trunk. Other trees are Texas red oak, escarpment live oak, cedar elm, and hackberry.

Flowering trees might include Texas mountain laurel, Mexican buckeye, rusty blackhaw viburnum, evergreen sumac, prairie flameleaf sumac, Texas persimmon, Texas redbud, Mexican plum, or bumelia. All these small trees are also sometimes classified as large shrubs.

Smaller thicket shrubs are elbowbush, aromatic sumac, and coralberry.

Flowers in the shade are likely to be baby blue-eyes, zexmenia, and cedar sage, often with short, grasslike cedar sedge.

Flowers in the sun are commonly bluebonnets, Indian blanket, and greenthread, plus a few dozen other species. Grasses are primarily little bluestem, sideoats grama, silver bluestem, buffalograss, and speargrass. In hollows or by creeks there might be big bluestem, Indiangrass, switchgrass, and Lindheimera's muhly.

Arguably the most beautiful part of the Lone Star State, the Hill Country is home to the famous bluebonnets, the official state flower of Texas. An escarpment live oak, green all winter, has just lost its leaves and is in the process of getting new ones. In the background is the juniper–Texas red oak scrub typical of this part of the Hill Country. A wealth of Ice Age relics hang on in the canyons, where they are safe from fire, sheep, and goats.

Canyons and stream banks are often covered with endemic or Ice Age relics. The tragedy is that this area is being subdivided into small lots at an alarming rate, although the Sierra Club has designated it one of the earth's most special places. The whole area from Round Rock south to San Antonio and west to Fredericksburg and Kerrville is rapidly becoming just more typical suburbia with St. Augustine lawns. There are few public parks here and no national parks, so even if every rancher were forced by high taxes to sell out, and even if homes were not built on large lots and on the envelope, *this extraordinary habitat could become virtually extinct within twenty years.*

Sandhills near Columbus, South Carolina

The sandhills are just that—sandy hills so dry that they have completely different vegetation from the lush habitats next door to them. The sandhills are becoming suburbia, but conventional methods of gardening are impossible here without tremendous wastage of water. The main vegetation on sandhills is a savanna habitat called turkey oak-longleaf pine barrens. "Barrens" is an old-fashioned name for land that is not fit for agriculture.

The longleaf pines grow to be about 100 feet tall, and the turkey oaks are the main understory tree, sometimes seventy-five feet tall, but usually much shorter. Turkey oaks turn brilliant red in November and it's a stunning sight. Their large red leaves are visually sandwiched between evergreen pines above and mostly evergreen shrubbery beneath. Other common trees are blackgums, which also turn red, and persimmons, which turn golden orange.

Tall shrubs, or flowering trees, are sparkleberry with its tiny white bells, deer-berry (a form of blueberry), and bristly locust with its pink wisteria-like blooms, plus many other plants such as sweetleaf, redbay, and American holly.

Knee- to waist-high shrubs are mountain laurel, wild rosemary, St. Andrews cross, dwarf huckleberry, sand myrtle, and a shrubby goldenrod. The main flowering season is from July through September, and these shrubs show pink, white, yellow, and gold. Accents are a low-growing, gold-and-lime flowered prickly pear and a sturdy yucca called Spanish bayonet.

The ground layer consists of wiregrass and broomsedge in the sun and bracken fern in the shade. Wildflowers in blue, purple, rose, pink, white, and yellow bloom daintily from spring to frost. To maintain a dense stand, wiregrass needs to be burned every three years.

Reindeer lichen and sand spikemoss, only an inch or so high, are the pioneer plants that carpet the sand and hold it well enough for the flowers, grasses, pines, and oaks to take root.

Deserts

If your image of desert is the Sahara or the Gobi, with vast stretches of sand and camel caravans, then the United States doesn't really have any deserts. But most authorities say we do, defining them as areas that lose more moisture to evaporation than they receive in snow or rain. The Great Basin Desert is also called sage scrub or sage steppe. It is found in flat areas below the piñon and juniper forests in Nevada, Utah, northern Arizona, northern New Mexico, and southwestern Colorado. It receives 60–70 percent of its moisture from snowmelt. Dominated by sagebush *Artemisia tridentata*, the spaces between the sage are filled with other waist-high shrubs as well as knee- to ankle-high grasses and flowers. Where salt has accumulated in the soil, shrubs such as shadscale are prominent.

The warm deserts are generally divided into the Chihuahuan, the Sonoran, and the Mojave. They all have creosote bush and ocotillo. At present, there is lots of bare earth or desert pavement (a fragile crust of small rocks) surrounding each plant, but historically there seems to have been a lot more grass cover.

The easternmost warm desert—and the coldest—is the Chihuahuan Desert, which extends from central New Mexico to north central Mexico. It is characterized by numerous species of cacti, tree yuccas, and agaves, as well as mesquite, acacias, mimosas, and cenizos *Leucophyllums*.

The Sonoran Desert, encompassing Phoenix, Tucson, and Yuma, Arizona, also extends south along Mexico's western coast. It is home to Desert Highlands (see chapter 8) and many other building envelope developments in southern Arizona. It is most famous for its saguaro cactus, paloverde trees, brittlebrush, and bursage.

The Mojave Desert is squeezed between the Great Basin and the Sonoran deserts, and its boundaries are blurred. Its dominants are creosote bush, bur sage,

sage bush, and shadscale. Some scientists question whether it is truly a separate desert, but 25 percent of its total species and 80 percent of its 250 annuals are found only there.

Mojave Desert near Las Vegas, Nevada

In the city itself, there are beautiful Torrey mesquites and creosote bushes along the Colorado River drainageway. But near Red Rock, Joshua tree, really a tall yucca with a "trunk," is the tallest plant. It is only six to ten feet tall at lower elevations, but at 3,500 to 5,000 feet in elevation, where it grows best, it might be over thirty feet tall.

Next in height are the banana yuccas and Mojave yuccas. Their large, white, waxy flowers, sometimes striped with pink or purple, are spectacular. Their sword-shaped leaves, like those of the Joshua tree, are evergreen.

Lots of thornless knee-high shrubs give year-round colors of gray-green, olive green, yellow-green, and khaki tan. After rains, they blossom. Creosote has yellow flowers, and its distinctive scent is a favorite with desert dwellers. Apache plume has white flowers and pink plumes of seed. Globe mallow has translucent cups of orange. Rabbitbrush covers itself with bright golden clusters in the autumn. Winterfat glows with silvery seed all winter. Other typical shrubs, some of them

The Mojave Desert (elevation 3,000–5,000 feet) averages just four inches of rainfall annually. Summer temperatures of 120°F are not unusual. Las Vegas and Bullhead City, Nevada, and Lancaster, California, are the main cities.

thorny, are bursage, blackbrush, wolfberry, goldenhead, dalea, Mormon tea, ratany, and hopsage.

Cacti are not common here and are very slow growing, so these spiny plants with bright-colored flowers are important to preserve. Beavertail, cholla, and barrel cactus are the larger ones.

Between the shrubs and cacti, there is still plenty of bare ground. In spring, this ground is sometimes covered by hundreds of short-lived wildflowers that blossom in shades of pink, yellow, and white. Clumps of grass lend a softness to the desert. Bush muhly, big galleta, and various needlegrasses are the most common.

Deciduous Forest

Deciduous forest is dominated by trees that lose their leaves in the winter. Considered to be the most diverse and species-rich habitat in North America, nearly seventy different trees and shrubs combine to make many subtle habitats across eastern North America. These habitats still cover about 11 percent of the continent, although they usually exist in somewhat damaged condition; logging and development have brought in many invasives.

Paradoxically, eastern deciduous forests are at least 50 percent white pine, red pine, Virginia pine, or loblolly pine. These pines, which are conspicuously nondeciduous, are now numerous because they are the traditional early succession Band-Aids for eastern deciduous forests after disturbance. Almost all eastern forests have been disturbed in the last hundred years.

Mature, dry deciduous forests are composed primarily of oaks and hickories, and many of these forests were savannas when they were burned regularly by lightning or Native Americans.

Moister deciduous forests used to be dominated by oaks and chestnuts. The American chestnut is now extinct for all practical purposes. A parasite from Asia (*Endothia parasitica*), which was accidentally introduced on the European chestnut around 1900, never lets the resprouts grow more than a few inches tall. American elm is also beleaguered in northern deciduous forests, although it is still common, along with other elms and ashes in deciduous midwestern creek woodlands.

Some of the oldest and lushest deciduous forests are a complex mixture of American beech, tulip tree, basswood, sugar maple, buckeye, red oak, white oak, and a dark green evergreen conifer called eastern hemlock. These beautiful forests have at least three layers of woody plants and a ground layer of ferns and delicate woodland wildflowers called "ephemerals" that bloom before all the trees are leafed out.

Maple-Basswood Forest in the Northern Midwest

This immensely complex and stately type of deciduous forest used to be prevalent throughout the northeastern United States. I've personally seen examples in Pennsylvania and Indiana. There are about forty acres left in southeastern

DOLLARS AND CENTS BENEFITS

There are numerous direct and indirect economic advantages to preserving, as well as restoring, native plant communities. Homes and other buildings situated in mature woodlands, as an example, cost less to heat and cool. Fred Buxton, a Texas architect, says that one of the office complexes he designed inside a tall conifer forest in Houston—where summers are often likened to steam baths—experienced savings of as much as 30–50 percent.

Landscaping and grounds maintenance are, of course, dramatically reduced. A study conducted by the Conservation Design Forum in Naperville, Illinois, discovered that restoring a habitat community with native plants significantly reduces installation and maintenance costs. Factoring in all the direct costs of such a restoration—such as ground preparation, planting, irrigation, weeding, fertilization, and core aeration—the costs of installing and maintaining a natural landscape over a ten-year period could be one-fifth that of maintaining a traditional lawn-centered landscape. Another study conducted by Applied Ecological Services in Brodhead, Wisconsin, estimated that the expense of maintaining a natural prairie or wetland over a period of two decades would be

COST OF INSTALLATION AND MAINTENANCE OF NATIVE VS. NON-NATIVE SPECIES

SITE PREPARATION	SODDED NON-NATIVE TURF GRASSES	SEEDED NON-NATIVE TURF GRASSES	NATIVE PRAIRIE OR WETLAND SEEDING
Spraying[1]	$140	$140	$140
Irrigation[2]	1,680	1,680	——
Topsoil[3]	4,480	4,480	——
Tilling	392	392	392
Sod & sodding	5,964	——	——
Seed & seeding	——	1,064	1,232
Wildflower planting[4]	——	——	1,680*
First year mowing	784	672	196
Total installation per acre[5]	$13,440	$8,428	$1,960– $3,640
Subsequent annual upkeep per acre	$1,120	$1,120	$168

1. Spraying must be done on site for live, undesirable vegetation such as quack grass, thistle or other noxious weeds
2. Cost of irrigation assumes an underground automatic system.
3. Topsoil is figured at approx. 3-inch depth hauled in from off-site
4. Wildflower planting is optional on low-profile site. The figure is based on 1,000 seedlings planted per acre.
5. Annual maintenance for turf grass includes 12 mowings per year plus fertilizer and irrigation. Annual maintenance for prairie/wetland includes annual burns and occasional spot spraying or mowing.

SOURCE: Applied Ecological Services, Inc.

approximately $2,000 an acre, while a conventional landscape would cost $3,000 an acre.

Other dollars-and-cents savings include reduced costs for storm water management; greater opportunities for recreation; reduced air, water, and noise pollution; and soil conservation. Natural features such as river corridors, prairies, wetlands, and woodlands are community assets that enhance property values.

Minnesota. The list below was developed from a study of those Minnesota "big woods" remnants. A maple-basswood habitat is typically about 100 feet tall.

The canopy trees are sugar maple and basswood (American linden). American elm was also a dominant species before it was destroyed by Dutch elm disease. Northern red oak and green ash are frequent components. The continuous canopies of these tall trees create a natural greenhouse of cool, calm, moist, filtered sunlight.

Fairy candles Cimicifuga racemosa *bloom in midsummer under deciduous forest canopy in the southern Appalachians. White flowers are best for attracting pollinators in dense shade. The flowers start blooming at the bottom of the spike and continue for several weeks. Underneath the lacy foliage of the fairy candles, ephemeral spring wildflowers have already gone to seed and disappeared under the thick blanket of decaying leaves dropped each autumn by the canopy trees. Here the dominant trees are maple, tulip poplar, and basswood.*

Their fallen leaves decompose to create a soil that is rich in organic matter, spongy with moisture, and full of dead air pockets that buffer changes in temperature.

The understory trees are composed of saplings of the canopy trees, as well as bitternut hickory, black cherry, butternut (a walnut), paper birch, and ironwood *Ostrya virginiana*.

Tall shrubs are beaked hazelnut or pagoda dogwood.

The ground layer is especially diverse and beautiful. Common forest herbs are bloodroot, yellow violet, large-flowered bellwort, wild ginger, northern maidenhair fern, and jack-in-the-pulpit. Spring ephemeral flowers that can occur in showy masses of white are false rue anemone *Isopyrum biternatum*, white trout lily, and Dutchman's breeches.

When the canopy is disturbed by the death of one tree, a sapling quickly grows up to fill in the gap. If logging occurs, harsh sunlight destroys the delicate understory plants. Native thorny shrubs spring up as Band-Aids—gooseberry, raspberry, and blackberry—as well as prickly ash, a small tree with large thorns. Bur-fruited herbs such as enchanter's nightshade, sweet cicely, and honewort also discourage people from disturbing the recovery program. If the soil is compacted by vehicles or too much foot traffic, wood nettle, normally found only on clay, springs up to protect the site until leaf litter and aeration are reestablished.

Nowadays, two exotic invasive shrubs, common buckthorn and Tartarian honeysuckle, are more likely to overtake disturbed sites, along with that much-hated exotic biannual garlic mustard. These need to be removed by burning, digging, or poisoning, as they prevent natural succession from taking place.

Norah Pierson and Frank Lloyd Wright would
have understood each other perfectly. The famed architect once said, "No house
should ever be built *on* a hill. It should be *of* the hill, belonging to it, so hill and house
could live together each the happier for the other."

In 1987, Norah purchased land in Lamy, New Mexico. The site was distinctive in
many ways, not the least being the petrified sand dune that dominated the property.
It was atop this dune that she planned to build her home.

Because she wanted her home to blend into the dramatic landscape—to be of the
dune and "disappear as much as possible"—she chose an unusual form of construction. Her 2,300-square-foot home was built atop the petrified sand dune and,
while the wooden frame of the five-level abode was conventional, the outer shell of
the house was not. Over a "form" of wood and chicken wire, she sprayed polyure-
thane foam, giving the exterior a rocklike appearance. The finished home looks like
the rock it sits upon and mimics the landscape.

Earth shelter homes have a long history; in China, towns and villages in the
loess, or silt, belt have been constructed underground for centuries. Because of the
softness of the soil, homes are carved twenty-five to thirty feet deep into the earth,

Norah Pierson's home in Lamy, New Mexico, sits atop a petrified sand dune and was designed to be, in the words of Frank Lloyd Wright, not on it but of it.

keeping them warm in winter and cool in summer. This ancient technique is still utilized today, with over ten million people living in these earth shelter dwellings.

Living intimately with our natural surroundings, of course, is not new. Perhaps the very first such abodes were tree-nests on the African savannas, similar to the ones still made by gorillas and other primates. Darwin observed chimpanzees in Africa and orangutans in Asia constructing "platforms" in trees, and these inspired our ancestors to do likewise. Later, our foreparents moved into caves, then into shelters constructed of skins and branches, and then log cabins and houses made of mud and stone.

In his delightful book *Architecture Without Architects*, Bernard Rudofsky points out that "untutored builders ... demonstrate an admirable talent for fitting their buildings into the natural surroundings. Instead of trying to 'conquer' nature, as we do, they welcome the vagaries of climate and the challenge of topography. Whereas we find flat, featureless country most to our liking (any flaws in the terrain are easily erased by the application of a bulldozer), more sophisticated people are attracted by rugged country."

Like Norah Pierson, many of them chose veritable aeries as building sites, and Rudofsky lists the ancient cities of Machu Picchu in Peru and Monte Albán in Oaxaco, Mexico, as well as the craggy monks' bastion on Mount Athos in Greece,

Nestled into the earth, earth shelter homes—sometimes called earthships—are now found all over the world. Many are built from recycled auto tires filled with compacted earth, while others are constructed of more conventional materials. Insulated by the earth, the homes have amazingly low heating and cooling costs. One earth shelter homeowner in Texas told me that it cost him less than $30 to heat and cool his home all year. Solar panels, cisterns, and winter sun–facing windows are common fixtures on many of these homes.

as classic examples. In this country, we can look at ancient Native American cliff dwellings at sites such as Mesa Verde in Colorado.

It was not until fairly late in our development, in the eighteenth century, that the more genteel segments of society began to look at nature not as a threat or a challenge but in more romantic and idealized terms. The upper classes, particularly in England, were no longer stay-at-homes, and a popular pastime was taking invigorating hikes through the wilder regions of Great Britain and the Continent, often bringing their sketchbooks and painting easels along to capture these new sights. They then retreated back to the comforts of their manor homes. The idea of actually living in such surroundings was, well, for the lower classes!

In many cases, landscape architects and engineers were hired to re-create the wilderness around these estates. A Lord Shelburne had a waterfall constructed on his estate at Wiltshire; it was located at one end of the artificial lake he had commissioned earlier.

The idea of actually choosing to live in a natural setting came from Asia, not Europe. Centuries before Europeans began to appreciate nature for aesthetic and philosophical reasons, fueled largely by Jean Jacques Rousseau's Romantic move-ment, homes were being built in natural settings throughout Japan and China. There, priests and scholars were able to think their deep thoughts in the serenity of these wild places, and many old drawings survive that depict these idyllic scenes.

One of the earliest examples of a European home built into the wilderness for aesthetic reasons was a cottage believed to have been designed by John Nash around 1820. Called the Swiss Cottage, it was built for the Earl of Glengall in southern Ireland, and it sat in the midst of a woodland overlooking the River Suir. Rustic, with a thatched roof and quaint verandahs, it also featured expensive French wallpapers and handsomely engraved glass windows, no doubt so that Lord Glengall would not forget his social position.

Two later—and far grander—examples were the works of British architect Richard Norman Shaw. In the 1870s, he designed Leyswood in Sussex and Crag-side in Northumberland, making them a part of their rocky surroundings.

While he might well be called a trailblazer in his field, few other architects fol-lowed Shaw's lead. Whenever new homes were built in wild areas during this pe-riod, they were situated high above their surroundings, on cliffs and promontories, reflecting the attitudes of the owners who saw themselves as standing far above the rest of society. Besides, in those times it was considered unhealthy to be closed in by woodlands.

THE CABIN IN THE WOODS

America too was experimenting with building in natural areas. One of the earliest and best-known examples is the simple cabin at Walden Pond built by Henry David Thoreau outside Concord, Massachusetts, in 1845. "I went to the woods," he wrote, "because I wished to live deliberately, to front only the essential facts of life and see if I could not learn what it had to teach, and not, when I came to die, discover that I had not lived." He built his cabin—ten feet wide by fifteen feet long by eight feet high—himself, at a cost of $28.12½.

Thoreau grew up with a passion for the great outdoors, writing in later years that nature was something "my spirit seemed so early to require." He had been greatly influenced at an early age by the writings of Ralph Waldo Emerson, a Unitarian minister, essayist, and founding member of the transcendentalist move-ment in New England. Emerson's essay "Nature" had an especially profound effect on the young Thoreau and in years to come the two became fast friends.

Thoreau was moved by Emerson's view of the natural world as an intricate tap-estry, which Emerson called "the web of God." During the two years (1845–1847) that he lived in his cabin at Walden Pond, Thoreau became a prolific writer, jotting down his thoughts and observations on a wide range of subjects, from civil disobe-dience to the economics of living a simple life not "frittered away by detail."

But the core of his writings was mankind's relationship to nature. His most fa-

For two years, 1845–1847, the famous writer and philosopher Henry David Thoreau lived a solitary but creatively fulfilling life in his cabin in the woods at Walden Pond. Even then, it was one of the few remaining woodlands in the heavily farmed area. Today this replica stands at the Walden Pond State Reservation in Concord, Massachusetts, and receives many thousands of visitors annually.

mous work, *Walden*, sold only a few thousand copies in his own lifetime. But in the years to come his genius was fully appreciated, influencing generations and turning them to a greater appreciation of nature and the nature of humankind—among them, John Muir, E. B. White, Mahatma Gandhi, Supreme Court Justice William O. Douglas, and the Reverend Martin Luther King Jr. Rachel Carson, whose *Silent Spring* alerted the world to the dangers of pesticides, kept a copy of *Walden* at her bedside.

RETREATS AND INNS

As the railroads spread across the land, prosperous vacationers were able to visit far-off wilderness areas and appreciate their rugged beauty. Naturally, when they got there, they had to have some place to stay, and primitive tents and campfire meals would not do. In 1823, Charles Beach, an entrepreneur and self-proclaimed naturalist, built a hotel—the Catskill Mountain House—on the edge of a cliff in the heart of the New York State mountain range, leaving the surrounding landscape virtually unaltered. But then he had the Otis Elevator company install a lift along the cliff face, which resulted in massive scarring of the mountain that is still visible today. The Catskill Mountain House, which continued in business for over a century—although the last decades were a struggle—became famous and was celebrated in poems and paintings.

By the early 1900s, the concept of building vacation homes and resorts into nat-

This engraving, done by Harry Fell in 1870, shows the famous and luxurious Catskill Mountain House atop its rocky promontory in the Catskills. In 1930 the property was purchased by the state, and the once elegant hotel gradually fell into ruin. In 1963, the New York State Conservation Department burned it to the ground. (Courtesy of Black Dome Press, Inc., Hensonville, N. Y., from The Catskill Mountain House, *by Roland Van Zandt)*

ural settings was becoming very popular. The work of Norman Shaw in England was being reflected in new constructions along the New England coastline. Summer homes were dotting the rocky shores and, in keeping with the trend toward being more natural, boulders were often incorporated into the foundations and were left strewn about the grounds.

The mountain vacation retreat of William A. Read was featured in a 1907 issue of *House & Garden* magazine, while the pages of *Sunset*, *Country Life*, and *Craftsman* sang the praises of many others. And resorts such as Kamp Kill Kare in the Adirondacks and Long's Peak Inn in Estes Park, Colorado, became regular stops on the vacation itineraries of the rich and famous. While these woodland settings were rustic, the accommodations and service were not. And while Thoreau may have preached and practiced "simplicity, simplicity, simplicity," visitors to these natural areas—including the likes of the Vanderbilts, Morgans, and Huntingtons—did not want their exposure to the simple life to be too simple. In *Durant: The Fortunes and Woodland Camps of a Family in the Adirondacks*, Craig Gilborn described the amenities of Kamp Kill Kare as it was in the winter of 1899: "Inside the bright fires blazed from great stone fireplaces, and the table was spread with all the delicacies one would expect to find at Delmonico's."

FALLINGWATER

Ask strangers to cite an example of a home integrated perfectly into its natural setting and the odds are good that they will mention Fallingwater. They may not call

it by name (often people refer to it simply as "that Frank Lloyd Wright house that sits on a waterfall") and they may not know that it is in southwestern Pennsylvania. But they will be able to describe it, for it has been photographed countless times. Even people who know nothing about architecture and little about Wright himself are familiar with this house that many call Wright's masterpiece. Thousands of visitors from all over the world come to see it every year, and readers of the *Journal of the American Institute of Architects* voted it the best American building of the past 125 years.

Fallingwater was famous even before it was completed in 1939, not merely because of who was building it but because it was viewed as a rare combination of technical genius and art.

The home was commissioned by Edgar J. Kaufmann, a wealthy Pittsburgh department store owner. He and his wife, Liliane, met Wright in 1934 when they visited his Taliesin Fellowship in Spring Green, Wisconsin. Their son, Edgar Kaufmann Jr., who would later write the definitive account of the home's history, *Fallingwater*, was at that time studying there under Wright's tutelage.

Kauffman was impressed by the famous architect's own home at Taliesin, situated in the rolling woodland hills of Wisconsin, and by the devotion of his apprentices. Soon, he and Wright formed a friendship based on mutual respect. As Kaufmann Jr. wrote, "Wright and my father were both outgoing, winning, venturesome men, and father quickly felt the power of Wright's genius."

Initially, the Kaufmanns had envisioned a vacation retreat alongside the waterfall on Bear Run, the stream that ran through their mountain property. Within the year, Wright visited the property. "Wright was led down old stone steps to a flat expanse of rock at the base of the falls," the younger Kaufmann recalled in his book. "Looking up Wright must have been fascinated by the torrent pouring over the fractured ledge; he saw a great opportunity for architecture." The waterfall, Wright realized, was the heart of the property; therefore, the home would not sit beside the falls but over it.

After commissioning Wright, Kaufmann waited many weeks for drawings to arrive but heard not a word from the architect. When Kaufmann could stand it no longer, he phoned Wright and said he'd be coming up to Taliesin for a look at the plans for his country home. Wright responded cheerily, "Come along, E.J. We're ready for you." In fact, according to several of Wright's apprentices, not a line had been drawn!

Later, Kaufmann phoned to say that he was less than two and a half hours away. Hearing that, Wright sat himself down at his drafting table and, in a rush of inspiration, began creating the home. His pencil flew and his ideas came at a furious pace. By the time Kaufmann drove up to the front entrance, Wright was there to greet him with detailed drawings for the first floor, the second floor, elevations, side views ... the works. In fact, Wright had not only designed the home, he had named it—Fallingwater. The basic design never changed.

As Kaufmann Jr. says in his book, "The man-made parts of Fallingwater would be incomplete without the natural setting." The interaction of site and building is inspired; the character of stone outcroppings is echoed in the walls of the house. Large boulders were incorporated into the structure, and several venerable oaks were interwoven into the design of the house, where they stand to this day.

Other trees and vegetation did not fare as well, however, and photos taken during the building phase show no evidence of protective fencing or other means of shielding them from the perils of construction work. The woodland that enfolds the house today is largely the result of allowing the land to heal itself and revegetate naturally.

When you look at a newly completed home
that was built using nature's envelope, it is often difficult to tell that the home is, in
fact, new. Instead of a broad, cleared band of earth surrounding the foundation,
native vegetation grows in close proximity to the structure. Trees, many decades
old, can be just a few feet away. The landscape looks established and mature—because it is. It has been left virtually undisturbed, looking, in the words of one architect, "as if a giant hand had gently set it down into the landscape."

What a contrast to new homes built with conventional methods, whose property requires a long recovery period. The few saplings and young foundation
plantings that may have been installed are years away from maturity. And, in most
cases, they have little to do with the native vegetation that had once occupied the
site.

The two principal misconceptions about nature's envelope voiced by those who
have not had any experience utilizing this technique are (1) it's got to be difficult
and (2) it's got to be expensive. Both notions are wrong.

I have spoken with a number of builders and architects who work with nature's
envelope, and in each case the process varies a bit. The following steps are a compi-
lation of the best executions that I either have seen firsthand or learned of from the

Envelope home north of Houston, Texas. The stone path marks where a fence protected the natural area during construction. This woodland is composed of native oaks and an understory of devil's walking stick, yaupon holly, and American beautyberry. Alongside the house, native sensitive fern and wood fern, and nonnative Asian azaleas had to be replanted because this area was destroyed during construction.

homeowners or builders. Whether you are a developer who has many acres to work with or an individual who is thinking of purchasing some land on which to build a dream home, these steps should provide ample guidance. You may have to adapt these steps to your specific situation.

One adaptation may concern the subject of lawns. Many envelope communities, such as the ones described in chapter 8, prohibit lawns altogether. Others restrict lawn size, primarily for reasons of water conservation. The neighborhood association to which my wife and I belong in New Mexico, for example, allows a maximum of just 100 square feet of lawn per each three-acre property. As it happens, only one neighbor actually takes advantage of this.

If you are attracted to the idea of preserving natural habitat yet still feel a need to have some portion of your property devoted to turf grass, clearly you will have to settle in a location where this is possible. The envelope is, after all, designed to preserve as much natural landscape as possible; how much you choose to preserve is up to you.

THE PLANT SURVEY

You've purchased your land. But do you really know what it is you've bought? It's a lot more than dirt and dimensions. It is a habitat full of flora, most of which is probably foreign to you. If you were thinking about purchasing a business, you would first want to know all about the personnel and the facilities, in short, all the assets and liabilities. Think of the habitat in those terms.

You may want to begin with a plant survey, or inventory, and to do this, you will undoubtedly need professional assistance. More on that later. The survey will determine the overall health and viability of the natural setting. It will also help in siting the house and driveway. You may think you know where you want the house, even though it would mean cutting down a dozen or so healthy trees. The survey may tell you that there are a number of old, diseased trees on the other side of the lot and that by moving the house ten feet over you can save the healthy young ones. You may also discover some rare and endangered plants on your land that will need to be protected. Without the survey, they might be overlooked and trampled.

The plant survey should do more than merely list the flora by name (both common and Latin); it should also give you a fairly good description of them so you can find them on your own and know something about their growth habits and the general condition of the plants—age and health. We recommend getting a few photo albums and pressing leaves and flowers under the plastic overlays, along with the names. Have one album for woody plants and another for ground layer flora. If your land is recovering rather than pristine, you may need a third album just for weed identification. Your county extension agent or a local nursery can help you identify these intruders.

Let's say your property is in the eastern United States, zones 5–8, and among the many plants growing there are black oaks. Under the general category of trees, that entry might look something like this:

TREES:
    COMMON NAME: Black oak
    LATIN NAME: *Quercus velutina*
    QUANTITY: 7 (5 being 40–60 feet tall, 2 under 12 feet)
    HEALTH: good
    Produces both attractive spring and fall coloring
    Soil on property is dry and acid—good for this species
    Taproot and deep-growing lateral roots, so young ones should not be
        transplanted
    Acorns attract birds, small mammals; larval plant for Juvenal's duskywing
        butterflies

If your property is in either the Chihuahuan Desert (El Paso, Las Cruces) or the Sonoran Desert (Phoenix, Tucson, Yuma), an entry night look like this:

CACTI:

    COMMON NAME: Fishhook barrel cactus

    LATIN NAME: *Ferocactus wislizenii*

    QUANTITY: 14 mature specimens 2–5 feet tall

    HEALTH: 2 very old and in questionable condition, others healthy

    Displays yellow fruits, orange blooms in late summer

    Has hooked spines as protective mechanisms

    If transplanted, west side of cactus should be protected for first week or two to prevent sunburn

    Good wildlife plant

NOXIOUS WEEDS

The fact is, some of the plants on your property may not be worth saving. Some, in fact, ought to be pulled out or dug up for the overall good of the landscape; you may even have to resort to one of the least toxic herbicides, such as glysophate. Even some natives are undesirable, poison ivy, dodder, cockle burs, and bull nettle, to name a few.

If the land has been revegetated (abandoned farmland or pasture that has reverted to a natural state), there is a very real probability that it has been invaded by a variety of exotics best described as noxious weeds. Noxious weeds are plants that are alien to a geographical area and threaten natural and agricultural ecosystems. One of the greatest threats to our environment is also probably the least known or appreciated—the invasion of noxious weeds from all over the world. Some of these plants were brought to this country deliberately to be used as ornamentals or for erosion control; others got here by accident, for example, in a shipment of cattle feed.

This is not a new problem; by 1672, twenty-two foreign weeds were established in New England, including plantain and the ubiquitous dandelion, which came here from northern Europe, most likely in cattle feed. The first documented weeds arrived on the *Mayflower*, but it isn't unlikely that Christopher Columbus or early Norse explorers may have transported some to the New World as well.

To give you an idea of what a problem these invasives can be, let's look at water hyacinth. Native to South America, it was introduced to this country as an ornamental. In the 1890s, a gardener from Florida brought one home from the Louisiana Exposition and planted it in her backyard pond. Her water garden was soon overrun by water hyacinth, so she tore the plants out and threw them into the St. Johns River, which ran behind her home. Today, Florida spends many millions of dollars each year trying to rid its canals, rivers, and lakes of this highly invasive and destructive plant.

Other such invasives are common all over the country: crown vetch, Russian knapweed, Australian blue eucalyptus, purple loosestrife, Russian olive, kudzu, and

COMMON INVASIVES OF NORTH AMERICA

NAME	ORIGIN	REGION ATTACKED	DAMAGE	DESCRIPTION	CONTROLS
Bluegrass eucalyptus *Eucalyptus globulus*	Australia	Coastal California	Fire-prone litter, reduces biodiversity	Tall tree with shedding bark, waxy blue leaves	Glyphosate applied to stump surface of cut trees
Chinese tallow a.k.a. Popcorn tree *Sapium sebiferum*	China	Gulf Coast up to North Carolina	Invades wetlands, bottomland forests	Medium-sized tree, heart-shaped leaves, clusters of waxy white seeds in fall	Hand-pulling of seedlings, systemic herbicides
Cotoneaster *Cotoneaster lacteus* *C. pannosus*	Eurasia, China	Central and northern California coast	Smothers sun-loving natives, reduces biodiversity	Shrubs with clusters of red berries in fall, white flowers in summer	Weed wrench when young, later 100% glyphosate on cut stumps
Crown vetch *Coronilla varia*	Europe, southwest Asia, north Africa	Northeast and Midwest	Outcompetes natives, degrades wildlife habitats	Low growing perennial with pink, lavender, or white blooms June–August	Shade out with heavy mulch or cloth. As last resort, chemicals
Norway maple *Acer platanoides*	Eurasia, northern Iran to southern Scandinavia	East coast, North-west, Canada	Outcompetes native sugar maples, beeches	Hand-shaped leaves, milky sap, smooth leaf underside	Urge planning boards to ban it as street planting. Pull seedlings, cut down mature trees
Purple loosestrife *Lythrum salicaria*	Eurasia	Northeast and Midwest	Threatens wetlands, rare native species, reduces food and shelter for wildlife	Tall growing perennial with long, showy purple spikes June–September	Hand pull before seeds set. Do not dig out; disturbed soil enhances spread
Russian olive *Elaeagnus angustifolia*	Europe, western Asia	Canada down through western states to northern Texas	Takes over riparian areas, choking out native willows and cottonwoods	Large deciduous shrub with silver-gray leaves, reddish bark	Pull out seedlings, cut larger ones and apply appropriate herbicide
Tamarisk *Tamarix ramosissima* *T. chinesis,* *T. parvoflora*	Mediterranean area, Middle East, China, Japan	All western states except Washington and North Dakota	Invades riparian areas, decreases biodiversity, eliminates food for wildlife	Tall shrubs or short trees with pink or white plumes spring through fall	Pull seedlings, treat mature plants by cutting, applying systemic herbicide to stumps

many more are running amok, crowding out native vegetation and throwing ecosystems out of balance. Because so many invasives are attractive, people find it difficult to think of them as threatening. Many are even being sold in nurseries. Chinese tallow is readily available in many Gulf Coast nurseries.

Clearly, then, your plant survey should not only identify the desirable plants but should target the undesirables as well. The plant survey should do more than merely list the flora by name (both common and Latin); it should also give you a fairly good description of what they look like so you can find them on your own, understand their growth habits, and recognize the general condition of the plants—age and health.

WHO SHOULD CONDUCT THE PLANT SURVEY?

Your first inclination may be to contact the professional plant people at your nearest nursery. But there's a risk in this; many nurseries primarily stock and sell exotic plants. Their knowledge of and experience with native flora can range from very limited to nonexistent. I have come across some nurseries that harbor a genuine dislike or—at the very least—suspicion of native species, and the "advice" they give can be counterproductive.

Today, there are many nurseries that specialize in native plants and, while their numbers are growing every day due to the increasing public demand for these plants, such nurseries tend to be regional. States such as Texas, Wisconsin, Minnesota, and parts of the Southwest have many such nurseries, although other states are just beginning to wake up to the advantages of going native.

County extension agents may or may not be helpful; some know their natives while others are woefully ignorant. The same can be said for landscape architects; most of their education deals with hardscapes: outdoor lighting, water features, irrigation systems, the construction of patios, walls, berms, and so on. Surprisingly, very little of their training—5 to 10 percent—actually deals with plants, and those are overwhelmingly common nursery stock (i.e., exotics).

To locate people who are knowledgeable about the indigenous flora of your region, contact your local native plant society, an arboretum that has regional native demonstration gardens, or some other related organization. (See the appendix.)

Other resources include a certified arborist (for the trees only); the Nature Conservancy, a national organization dedicated to preserving wilderness area; and the botany department of a local college or university. In many instances, botany departments per se are being absorbed into science or biology departments, as botany is losing favor in the academic community. If that's the case in your area, ask for a staff member who knows the local flora and can spare a few hours to walk your property. You will, of course, have to pay for this service (no matter who does it), but it will be money well spent if it enables you to rid your land of noxious weeds and identify the "keepers."

These keepers may include rare or endangered species you'll definitely want to save, as they will help maintain the biological diversity of your land, or they may have special aesthetic and wildlife value. The survey should also tell you which plants will be more resilient to the disturbances that construction activities will cause.

Your property may also be home to some especially grand specimens that may have historic value. These would be irreplaceable and should not be considered "renewable resources." As Jim Wilson and Guy Sternberg point out in their book *Landscaping with Native Trees*, "Historic trees may have shaded important tribal gatherings or provided a backdrop for great orations. Their towering height may have been a landmark for competing armies … The rights of ownership carry social responsibility."

SELECTING THE ARCHITECT AND BUILDER

For the lay person planning a new home, especially for the first time, choosing an architect and a builder is always an important decision. But it is crucial when you are going to use the nature's envelope technique. Very likely, the architects and builders listed in your Yellow Pages will not have had any previous experience with this relatively new concept, so you will have to make your wishes and expectations very clear up front. It is not unreasonable to interview several candidates before you find the ones who are in tune with your ideas. It isn't vital that they have prior experience with the envelope; it is imperative that they understand it and feel enthusiastic about working with this technique.

If your architect is going to be involved through the final stages of construction, it is a good idea to get his or her input on the selection of the general contractor. The relationship between architect and builder had better be smooth or it can wind up costing you time and money and adding immeasurable stress to the project.

You might even consider selecting your landscape architect or designer and your architect at the same time and try to get them to work together from the very beginning. "Even," as a landscape architect friend says "if it hurts."

MARKING OFF THE FOOTPRINT

Once you have picked your architect, plan to walk through your property together, selecting the house and driveway sites (the footprint) so as to *make the least negative impact on the land*. Obviously, you can't build a house without altering the landscape significantly. The idea here is simply to save as much of the prime vegetation—and topography—as possible, while still getting the home you have in mind.

Slopes, interesting rock formations, arroyos and washes, natural swales and berms—like the plant materials—constitute a significant part of the character of the property. These will also help determine the location of the footprint, and a creative architect can suggest ways to incorporate these features into the overall design. At Fallingwater, Frank Lloyd Wright utilized the massive boulders as part of the foundation.

Because natural land, even "level" land, has drainage courses and slopes, a topographical survey, or "topo," will have to be made before the exact location of the footprint can be determined. Your architect or builder can suggest competent people to do this.

LONG-TERM EFFECTS

Another important consideration is determining how vegetation on your property is affected by rain runoff and snow melt. Particularly in arid zones, this can be an important part of the natural irrigation these plants have come to rely upon, and locating the house and other structures uphill from the plants can impede or even eliminate this source. Trees that you've taken pains to save up close to the house can, after a year or two, begin to look stressed because they are now getting less moisture than they've been accustomed to.

Again, some creative designing can help this situation; for example, if a veranda or patio abuts the trees, make sure rain can flow from this surface out to the trees. If a low wall is part of this structure, put flow through ports every ten feet or so. An outdoors water tap at that location can also make supplemental watering easier. Where tree roots have been significantly cut, you may need to water for a couple of years to help the tree reestablish an adequate root system.

This piñon sits just a few feet from the patio wall. Feeder roots were damaged during construction, and natural runoff was interrupted. During the first summer, the tree showed signs of stress, unlike the tree situated further away from the site. Giving it supplemental water for the next two years caused the piñon to rally and it is now doing very well.

Other factors you'll be considering are the relationship of the house to the sun (to take advantage of solar warmth in the winter months), views (not just scenic but of other houses on nearby properties), and, if relevant to your situation, locations for a well, a septic system with leach field, and utility lines. In every case, care must be taken to locate these in places where their installation will disturb the land and the plant materials as little as possible.

DIVIDING UP THE PROPERTY

On your plat, divide the property into three zones. Later you will mark them off by staking.

* The Private Zone, or the footprint, is composed of the house, driveway, parking area, and any other structures such as a patio, pool, and freestanding garage.
* The Natural Zone is that part of the property to be protected. It is composed of the vegetation and terrain features that inspired you to purchase this land in the first place.
* The Transition Zone is a 5–15 foot band that surrounds the footprint and separates the private and natural zones. The width varies depending on what needs to be done at any particular point. If this seems like a tight fit, remember that scaffolding is only five feet wide, so there should be ample elbow-room for the work crews to move about comfortably between the house and the protective fencing. Building materials can be stored where the garage and parking area will be. *The key to using the envelope effectively is to minimize the width of the transition zone as much as possible.*

This diagram depicts a typical lot full of natural vegetation. Before you decide where the house and driveway go, conduct a plant survey and find out what you have; what is worth keeping, what can be lost. Also take into consideration the natural lay of the land; preserve rock formations, slopes, arroyos—all the features that give character to the land—and place the building where it will have minimal impact on the property.

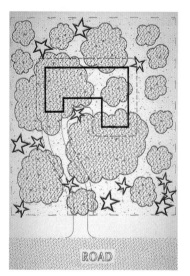

When you have decided where the house and driveway will be placed, draw a line five to fifteen feet around this footprint. This area between the footprint and the natural area to be preserved is the transition zone. At the outer edge of this transition zone, install a fence or barrier to keep workers and equipment from intruding into that space.

When construction is completed—and the barrier to the natural zone has been respected—you will have a home that looks as if it had been gently set down into the landscape without disturbing it. The transition zone will be relandscaped with vegetation salvaged prior to construction, so that the end result will be a seamless, very natural setting.

MARKING THE KEEPERS

One of the best tools for preserving your natural area is colored outdoor tape, available in most hardware stores. Get at least four rolls in four different colors. You'll need them as you decide which plants are to be kept where they are, which ones are to be moved to better locations, which ones to eliminate, and which ones to dig up for preservation off-site for later transplanting. It's not necessary, of course, to mark every single plant within the natural zone; as we'll soon see, there is a simpler method to ensure their safety.

You can, of course, begin marking plants during the initial plant survey, al-

*These cacti have been marked
for transplanting into the transition zone.*

though you may want to wait a bit while you digest the information and become
more familiar with the property. Perhaps the best time to tag plants is following
your walk-around with the architect when the three zones have been defined and
marked. As you tag the plants with the appropriate colors, make notes on your
plant survey report or in a notebook. You'll want to have a record of your deci-
sions should some of these ribbons become disengaged and blow away in the
wind.

The architect and builder, as well as the crews who will be doing the actual
work, should be made aware of the color code you are using, for example, red for
keepers, yellow for plants to be removed permanently, blue for plants to be removed for later transplanting. These colors, of course, are assigned arbitrarily, and
the last thing you want is a miscommunication on the significance of these colors
that results in a "keeper" being cut down by mistake.

FENCING OFF THE NATURAL ZONE

Before any actual construction begins, and especially before bulldozers or tree
spades arrive, erect a fence along the line defining the edge of the transition zone to
ensure that the natural zone will be well protected. The envelope is formed by the
fencing that protects the natural zone, *and everything involved in the actual construction takes place within the fencing.* The supplies and equipment are stored there, and
all the work takes place there. Again, it can't be stressed too much—nothing takes
place outside that fence.

RIBBON MARKERS

You've probably seen those bright yellow plastic ribbons that police departments
use to identify and cordon off crime scenes. The same type of ribbon is available
printed with "do not enter, protected vegetation area" in both English and Spanish

Chainlink fencing protects this natural Sonoran Desert landscape and still gives the construction crews ample room for working and storing materials and equipment. The type of fencing can vary from heavy chainlink to stretches of chicken wire to those orange plastic construction barriers to simple strands of clothesline, marked at intervals by colored ribbon. Clearly, the sturdier the fence, the more assurance there is that the integrity of the natural zone will not be violated.

Like a crime scene marker, this construction site ribbon reminds workers in both English and Spanish that the natural area beyond the fence is sacrosanct.

and can be ordered from Industrial Sign and Graphics, Charlotte, North Carolina, 800-824-7446. The tape comes in 1,000-foot rolls and is very inexpensive.

Run this ribbon around the top of the fence so no one can miss seeing it. Fencing off the natural zone means that *it is sacrosanct*. Nobody and nothing goes outside that barrier. Leftover concrete, paint, or plaster should be carted off site; they should never be allowed to run under the fence into the natural area. Workers should not even be allowed to eat their lunch there. For nature's envelope to work, this barrier must be respected and enforced.

CONTRACTS

Remember the famous line penned by the poet Robert Burns, "The best laid schemes of mice and men gang aft agley [often go astray]." This is really just Murphy's Law with a Scottish accent. But we've all been around long enough to know the truth of his admonition. Therefore, in any written agreements between the property owner and the builder (no handshakes or gentlemen's agreements here) there must be a clear understanding that the builder is financially responsible for any damage to the vegetation being protected on the property.

That means that if a mature tree is girdled and dies, it does not get replaced with a five-gallon sapling. Besides being an attractive part of the landscape, that tree provided shade, erosion control, and valuable habitat for songbirds and other critters. But transplanting an equally mature replacement, measuring anywhere from thirty to seventy feet high, just isn't practical. Not only would it be outrageously expensive, but it would require expertise that is not readily available and heavy equipment that would undoubtedly cause even greater damage to the property. In the 1920s, William Randolph Hearst is said to have had a venerable two-hundred year-old oak tree at San Simeon moved ten feet to one side simply because, in its original location, it was blocking his view. He brought in tree experts from Europe to supervise the move. It was an expensive proposition, but then he was William Randolph Hearst. The tree survived, by the way.

PUTTING VALUES ON THE PLANTS

Predetermined dollars-and-cents values need to be assigned to the major trees or other key vegetation, and those values ought to be written on price tags and affixed to the trees where they can be read easily by the subcontractors. These are not replacement costs because, as already noted, in many cases large, mature plants would be irreplaceable. Rather, *they ought to be considered penalties*, just as a jury would levy a dollar amount in a lawsuit involving personal injury. Then, should any of the workers or subcontractors inflict permanent damage on one of those plants, the builder is held liable for that amount. It's amazing how careful workers can be when they know that the boss will feel the consequences of their actions in his wallet.

Remember, the natural zone is protected, and no one should be in it in the first place. If the builder refuses to sign the liability agreement, take that as a red flag that he or she may not honor other agreements and get another builder.

THE PRICING FORMULA

If you have ever purchased a modestly sized tree for a home landscape—four- to eight-inch caliper—you know that, depending on the species and general condition, it can cost many hundreds of dollars. A typical cost is $100 per caliper inch, delivered, planted, and guaranteed. Trees above eight inches require greater labor and heavier equipment, and the cost goes way up. Then too the mortality rate of the trees rises precipitously. One nursery I contacted charges $1,700 for a seven-and-a-half-inch red oak, and $875 for a twelve- to fourteen-foot-tall yaupon holly.

Determining a fair "penalty" cost for a much larger mature tree is not a matter of taking an educated guess. And you can get different estimates, depending on who is doing the appraising. Would the owner of a lumber company and a poet view the value of a tree in the same way? Consider the following case. A landowner was about to lose two large oaks that were in the way of highway construction. To negotiate a fair price with the state, two foresters were called in. The first placed a value of $300 on each tree, based on the current price of firewood.

The other forester said the trees were worth $10,000 each! He used a formula devised by the Council of Tree and Landscape Appraisers (CTLA) and factored in, not the value of whatever products could be obtained from the trees but numerous other considerations, including size, condition, shade value, aesthetic value, site value (erosion control, privacy screening, light and glare shield, wind screening, importance to wildlife), rarity of the species, and historical value. If, for example, these oaks had been around when the area was first settled by Europeans or if they were treaty oaks or witness oaks, they would have added value. From yet another angle, that landowner might have proposed to his wife under those trees; does that get factored into the equation?

Clearly, placing a value on trees is not a simple matter and is not a job for amateurs. The people at the National Arbor Day Foundation recommend getting professional help. The CTLA formula is a big help, but it is subjective in many ways. So, just as with doctors, get a second opinion. (See the appendix for the CTLA address, as well as other appraisal references.)

SAVING VEGETATION IN THE PRIVATE AND TRANSITION ZONES

Before construction begins, the private and transition zones will have to be cleared, and conventional methods of bulldozing and chainsawing will be utilized. The reality is, perfectly healthy and beautiful trees will have to be felled because they are too large to deal with in any other way. But understanding this intellectually is not the same as experiencing it emotionally, and I've known property owners who made certain they were not around when the felling day arrived. The only way to handle this is to remember that you are saving a great deal of vegetation that would ordinarily have been lost. And then, of course, there's all that firewood you'll have for future cold winter nights.

But what about the plants inside those zones that are deemed worth saving? Smaller ornamental trees? Or, in a desert setting, a medium-sized saguaro or Joshua tree? They can be lifted out of the ground by tree spades, boxed, and put on drip irrigation to keep them healthy until construction is completed, when they can be used to revegetate the transition zone around the house.

Trees that sit where the house will go needn't be chain-sawed down; in many cases, they can be safely dug up using a tree spade, then boxed off-site and kept on a drip irrigatino line until they can be re-planted on the property after construction is completed.

The symbol of conventional construction

'DOZERS

Ask our friend Ron Nelson about bulldozers. Ron is an architect and while he may not claim to be an environmentalist, he loves nature and knows the importance of preserving a natural landscape. In 1986, he purchased an undeveloped half acre in Oak Cliff, Texas, on which he would design and build his personal dream home. The lot was full of trees and understory, most of which were native to the area.

The plot sloped down from the street at a precipitous angle, making access from the front a dicey proposition for the builder. The best solution would be to use the alley easement that ran behind Ron's property and several others. The lot next to Ron's had also been recently purchased, as it happened, by another architect. But inexplicably this architect did not know that the easement extended behind his land, so he instructed his bulldozer operator to cut across a corner of Ron's property. A number of healthy trees, as well as all the understory, were demolished. It took a court case to compensate Ron for his loss. But as he tells it, "That was only money. It couldn't replace the established vegetation that would take decades to regrow."

But that's not the end of the story. Ron's neighbor on the other side proposed a fence between the two properties. Ron agreed to split the cost but made it clear that he didn't want any of the vegetation destroyed in the process. He wanted a simple wooden fence that could be erected without unduly impacting the site. "Well," he says, "a bulldozer arrived one day when I wasn't around and cleared a wide swath down the property line, again destroying dozens of trees that I had counted on as a visual and sound buffer."

When the time came for Ron to begin construction of his own house, he made it very clear to his bulldozer operator what would and would not be fair game for the blade. "He was actually something of an artist," Ron recalls. "He handled that piece of equipment with the skill of a surgeon." But still Ron decided to be on hand whenever the 'dozer was in use. All went well until they broke for lunch, and Ron made the mistake of getting back to the site fifteen minutes later than the operator. "Two beautiful trees were already down!" he says. "No telling how many more would have gone down if I hadn't shown up."

Ron's experience is not unique. To paraphrase writer P.J. O'Rourke, "Putting some people at the controls of a bulldozer is like giving whiskey and car keys to teenaged boys."

This moving must be done by experienced personnel who understand the characteristics of the plants. Post oaks, for example, have very sensitive root systems and suffer a high mortality rate when transplanted, and saguaro cacti must always be kept in the same relationship to the sun that they grew up with. Care must also be taken not to overwater these plants.

Ground covers and small shrubs that would be inefficient to dig up and maintain on drip systems can still be saved. Contract with a local nursery to collect seeds and cuttings from these small plants and then grow them for you while the house is being built. By the time construction is completed, these plants should be ready to be replanted.

Leaving Trees Inside the Fencing

There will probably be at least one tree, shrub, or cactus that stands fairly close to the house (or to where the house will soon stand) that you'll want to save because it is very attractive and creates a very special accent. But, again, it is too large to dig up and transplant.

The builder may try to talk you into removing it, saying it is just too snug a fit for his people to maneuver around. In some cases that will be true. But in many cases, it can be saved by simply building a small protective fence around it and then taking a little extra time and care to work around it. The builder may rationalize removing it to save you the extra labor expense—time, as they say, is money! But a lot of time was involved in growing that tree in the first place, and that shouldn't be casually disregarded.

Hangovers

Often a tree will stand in the natural zone safely outside the fence, but the branches spread well into the building site. The temptation is to cut them off, leaving a lopsided tree that will never look right. This can be avoided by simply tying ropes to the branches and pulling them aside when that area needs to be accessed by the workers. Again, this is not a difficult thing to do, but it is rarely considered. It's so much easier to just lop off the intruding limbs.

SAVING THE TOPSOIL

A number of builders who work with nature's envelope scrape off all the topsoil inside the fence and pile it up off to one side, to be spread out again in the transition zone once the building is finished. If this seems like an unnecessary, even silly step, consider that this soil contains all the indigenous seeds and nutrients that compose the character of the land. Even desert soil or thin caliche should be preserved. It is, after all, what the indigenous plants grew in and it's the type of soil they are genetically adapted to.

Because of our long-established notions of conventional landscaping, we immediately want to truck in loads of outside topsoil. This may make us feel good, but it isn't what the local plants need or want. For example, desert plants do poorly in rich loam because they are genetically suited to well-drained limestone, sand, or decomposed granite. After all the trouble you went to save them, you could wind up killing them with kindness.

But there's another, equally important reason why you don't ever want to bring in outside topsoil. It is frequently full of unpleasant surprises, such as nutgrass, garlic mustard, thistles, and other noxious weeds that are almost impossible to get rid of. The supplier may offer you passionate assurances that his topsoil is pure; some have been known to boil or chemically treat their dirt, but this just kills off the vital microorganisms that keep soil healthy. In the end, you will probably spend the rest of your life pulling weeds that sprang up out of that "pure" soil.

COMMON PLANT-INJURING MISTAKES

Disease, old age, and lumbering are not the only causes of tree mortality. Frequently, trees that were intended to be saved die as a result of the things that happened to them during construction. In almost all cases, the deaths were unnecessary and avoidable.

My wife once received a panic call from a couple who had been in their new house less than a year. The property they had purchased had been largely stripped of natural vegetation, but the builder had left three large, well-established (and seemingly healthy) shade trees. In fact, these trees had been a major factor in the couple's purchasing decision. When Sally was contacted, one tree was already dead and the other two were terminally ill, although the couple didn't yet realize that.

She went out to see if anything could be done and quickly discovered what had happened. The construction crews had done a number of things, out of ignorance, that doomed these trees. Dirt had been piled up around the trunk of one tree—the one that had already died—and had covered the flare at the base. The flare should begin at ground level. Cause of death: suffocation.

The second tree died of starvation because the bark had been girdled by heavy equipment. Large patches had been scraped off, leaving the vital cambium, sapwood, and inner bark unable to function. The cambium is a microscopically thin layer of cells in which all growth occurs. The sapwood, or *xylem*, is the conduit through which water and nutrients rise to the leaves and branches. It also carries reserve food from storage cells contained in the roots. The inner bark, or *phloem*, is the conduit that carries sugar, hormones, enzymes, and other materials down to the roots and their storage cells.

Heavy equipment isn't the only thing to cause girdling. On one job site, I saw large and heavy flagstones leaning up against the thin bark of several trees. It's also not uncommon to see bricks, empty pallets, and heavy metal drums loaded

*On some proper-
ties, water wells
must be drilled.
Unless you have
an especially con-
scientious driller,
you may wind up
with delicious
fresh water—but
with considerable
damage to the
vegetation.*

with trash shoved up against the trunks. Thin-barked trees include aspens, beeches, and maples.

The third tree died because the roots were poisoned. We tend to think of tree roots as being very large and going very deep, not only collecting reserve water and minerals but anchoring the tree to the earth. But trees also have a vast network of fine roots inches below the surface, collecting water, nutrients, and oxygen. This network is vulnerable to harsh solvents, paints, and the washout from cement mixers. Certainly, no washouts or solvent dumping should be allowed under or even close to the dripline of the trees.

On a personal note: soon after my wife and I moved into our woodland home, we placed a salt lick about thirty feet from the house. Within six months we noticed that two piñons located five or six feet downhill from the lick were starting to look stressed. It took us a few minutes to realize that the salt lick was the villain. Rain and snow melt had been carrying salt down into the sensitive root system. We re-moved the salt lick and the trees recovered.

Roots can also be damaged when the soil is compacted under the dripline, either by parking vehicles or storing materials and heavy equipment there. In some cases, this can be avoided by constructing a simple platform bridge over the dripline when activity in that area is unavoidable and fencing off the tree is not possible.

Also, excavation too near the trunk cuts off far too many of the roots carrying nutrient flow. If the roots on one side of the tree are severely cut, the branches and leaves on that side will suffer, leaving a living but lopsided specimen. At first

There are any number of ways to damage vegetation during construction. Here, heavy flagstones are laid against tender bark, while on another site, the washout from the cement mixer gets into the soil and harms sensitive roots.

glance, a large shade oak or elm may look sturdy and impervious to anything we can do to it. Clearly, this is not true. Trees—especially the larger, older ones—are vulnerable and valuable, and they need our protection.

THE TRUE COST OF LAND-SCRAPING

One of the first questions I hear when I mention nature's envelope is, "How much does it cost to do all this?" The question is valid, and the answer is, not very much.

FIRE AND THE ENVELOPE

Whenever I speak on the envelope, someone invariably asks, "Doesn't building in the woods create a greater fire hazard for the homeowner?"

A reasonable question. But it strikes me that it may be rooted in something more basic than concern about increased insurance premiums. Fear of fire is primal and is undoubtedly rooted way back in our origins as a species, along with fear of snakes and fear of the dark. Interestingly, we don't seem to harbor the same anxieties about living in

flood plains, along earthquake faults, or in "tornado alley" in the Midwest. Moreover, we don't appear to be as concerned about any other causes of house fires: faulty cooking and heating equipment, smoking in bed, or combustible shake shingle roofs, to name a few. Of the many thousands of homes damaged or destroyed each year by fire—accounting for over $5 billion in property loss—the vast majority of these homes are surrounded by expanses of conventionally mowed lawns.

Still, the question must be addressed. And the answer is simple. Yes, living in the woods does increase the risk that your home may be lost to a forest fire. But how serious is that risk?

In most parts of the country—the Northwest, the Northeast, and Southeast—forest fires are rare, due to high humidity and rainfall. In the more arid portions of the country—especially California, where chaparral and forest fires seem to be a summer staple on the evening news—developers using the envelope technique can and should take certain precautions to reduce the risk.

1. Build in relatively mature woodlands with large, well-spaced trees and a high canopy.

2. Clear away deadwood and other combustibles surrounding the house, both ground debris and dead branches on trees and shrubs. Needles from conifers ought to be left alone; they benefit the habitat by replacing and renourishing the soil. A thick bed of needles will actually retard fire, whereas a thin layer will burn much too quickly to pose any real threat.

3. On the side of the house where winds are most likely to sweep a fire in your direction, create a fireguard—a patio or high masonry wall. And have ample water outlets installed.

4. If you plant trees in the transition zone, choose those that are less likely to burn. Trees high in oil, such as any of the Australian eucalyptus, ignite easily, while thick-barked oaks are designed by nature to withstand grass fires. Ironically, the popular blue eucalyptus, which is sold in nurseries despite the fact that it is highly invasive, litters the ground with twigs and papery bark just waiting for a hot spark.

5. Homeowners may elect to push the envelope line out farther from the house than the fifteen-foot maximum mentioned here. This of course involves a trade-off: destroying some of the natural habitat that the envelope is designed to preserve.

My wife and I live snugly in the piñon/juniper forests of northern New Mexico, and we understand that a forest fire is not impossible. In fact, a fire fierce enough to burn the crowns of the trees sprang up some six miles away in Lama while our home was under construction. On the positive side, annual snow melts and late summer rains have traditionally kept our forest reasonably "fire-resistant."

Then too all of us in our community work to reduce the risk of fire. When we are in a dry period, we have moratoriums on burning trash—the cause of that Lama fire—and campfires. Our volunteer fire department is well equipped, well trained, and well supported by our neighbors. In addition, the U.S. Forest Service annually issues permits to the public so they can gather firewood in the Carson National Forest. Locals pay $5 per cord to help the Forest Service thin trees where needed and clean up deadwood from the forest floor.

As this book is being written, the Community Forest Restoration Act, introduced by U.S. Senator Jeff Bingaman (D-NM), is making its way through Congress. This bill, designed to thin public forests and reduce the risk of wildfires, provides grants of up to $450,000 over a four-year period to fund collaborative projects between community organizations and tribal, state, and federal agencies. And, of course, let us not forget Smokey the Bear, who has been helping educate the public about preventing forest fires since 1944.

The degree of risk is determined by many factors. Does that risk outweigh the many benefits of living in close proximity to nature? We choose to live with a positive attitude, enjoying what we have instead of living in fear of what may never happen.

Gage Davis, the architect and landscape architect who pioneered this concept in Desert Highlands in Scottsdale, Arizona, back in 1983, estimates that utilizing nature's envelope adds approximately 5 percent to the total building costs. But, he quickly adds, that is normally more than offset by eliminating the considerable expense of relandscaping from scratch.

To find out how big a bite out of your building budget revegetating can take, University of Georgia graduate student Tamara Graham Calabria, under the supervision of Professor Darrel G. Morrison of the School of Environmental Design, studied a residential community under construction—Newpoint in Beaufort, South Carolina. The land in many areas was still undisturbed and full of native flora.

Analyzing a typical ten-meters-square plot, Tamara found a wealth of indigenous plant species—canopy trees, understory, ground covers, and wildflowers—over forty different species in all. (Contrast that to the five or eight plant species found in a typical suburban landscape.) She then determined the replacement cost of each plant, factoring in not just its size but the cost of installation: labor, mulch, fertilizer. Because she conducted her study in the winter, many of the dormant deciduous species were not included.

Sample replacement costs in 1994 (the year she conducted this study) included: $3.00 each for one- to three-foot redbays *Persea borbonia*, $12 for a four-quart bracken fern *Pteridium aquilinum*, $65 for a quarter- to half-inch caliper sweet bay magnolia *Magnolia virginiana*, and $900 for a six-inch caliper live oak *Quercus virginiana*.

The entire ten-meter-square area was found to contain plants with an estimated replacement value of

$5,750 for canopy trees (pines, hickories, oaks)
$2,840 for understory (shrubs, ornamental trees, etc.)
$9,825 for ground covers (bracken ferns, Virginia creeper, etc.)
Total $18,415

Projecting that figure to reflect the amount of landscaped area on the development's quarter-acre lots, the cost of replacing the native habitat becomes $58,500. Clearly, Tamara concludes, it is prohibitively expensive to re-create a comparably mature forest habitat once it has been cleared. It is far better to preserve the original landscape.

A copy of Tamara Calabria's report "The Landscape at Newpoint" can be obtained by contacting Rene D. Shoemaker, H. B. Owens Resource Center, School of Environmental Design, 609 Caldwell Hall, University of Georgia, Athens, GA 30602, (706-542-8292). E-mail rds@arches.uga.edu.

The house (or church or office building or
other commercial structure) is now completed and the temporary protective fencing has been removed. But all around the structure is that transition zone—five to
fifteen feet of bare space. Typically, the soil has been compacted and contaminated
in spots by concrete, paint, and other chemicals. You may have stuck to your guns
and saved a tree right up to the building, but aside from that all vegetation has disappeared, having been dug up and moved to a safe haven, cut down, or trampled
underfoot.

The job ahead of you is to revegetate this transition zone so that within a couple
of years it will show no sign of ever having been disturbed, and it will blend seam-
lessly into the preserved natural zone. This job is accomplished in seven steps:

1. clean up the soil
2. transplant the salvaged vegetation that requires a tree spade or other heavy
   equipment
3. aerate the soil
4. spread on the salvaged topsoil
5. plant the custom-grown vegetation and/or sow native seed

This native currant was salvaged from the roadside near the authors' home and replanted in the transition zone after construction was completed. All the vegetation that was introduced on the property is indigenous to the area. Transplants need a year or two of regular irrigation to get established, and then they should be able to fend for themselves.

6. mulch if appropriate
7. water until the vegetation is established and is ready to thrive on rainfall alone

CLEANING UP THE SOIL

The soil is the medium in which the plants grow, so its health is vital to their long-term health. For the revegetated area to fill in as quickly as possible and the new or saved plants to thrive there, the soil needs to be restored as closely as possible to its original condition. If, prior to construction, this soil had never been subjected to herbicides, fungicides, pesticides, and artificial fertilizers, as have most conventionally landscaped yards, it should be full of the kind of microorganisms (bacteria and algae) that define healthy soil. Just as our bodies contain billions of bacteria that keep us alive and healthy, these microorganisms keep soil healthy, breaking down organic matter and converting it into easily assimilated nutrition, and producing nitrogen.

It is important to remove all chemical spills as well as construction debris, such as dried concrete, bits of wood, and bricks, that would affect the texture and chemical composition of the soil. These substances need to be picked up and carted off to the dump. Latex paint spills, for example, will be congealed and bonded to the soil in sheets up to an inch thick. Some other spills, such as stucco, will form crusts that easily crumble. In either case, the whole mess should be lifted up with a spade and removed from the site. *Do not try to dilute the spills with water*; you'll just be spreading the noxious chemicals into fresh untainted soil.

This piñon was one of twenty-five salvaged from the authors' property. The nursery that dug up the trees kept twenty-two of them for the nursery's inventory, and replanted three others along the road to provide additional screening. The nursery made money selling the trees, so this operation didn't cost the authors a penny.

TRANSPLANTING LARGE SALVAGED VEGETATION

Large trees, shrubs, cacti, or other vegetation that you dug up with a tree spade and have been keeping watered and alive are now ready to be replanted. These large specimens are visually important, serving as accents in the landscape and making the transition zone appear more realistically a part of the whole; if all you had there was low-growing ground covers, the effect would look abrupt and unnatural.

Placing these larger plants around your house is rather like arranging furniture in a room. Both practicality and aesthetics come into play. Make up a list of the plants and walk around the house, looking at it from all angles. Where do you most

Unlike highway departments and many landscapers, Mother Nature does not work in straight lines and boxes. When revegetating, remember to keep the plant layout natural. But unlike a truly natural layout, yours can show evidence of aesthetic judgment. Place plants where you need an accent or a window shade, or just because it seems to belong in a certain spot.

need a large item to preserve the basic texture of the native landscape? Where do you most want a window shaded? What will make the front door seem welcoming?

Whatever you do, do not place these plants around the house in a measured, mathematically precise layout, one every six feet in a straight line. That's the way highway departments install trees and shrubs. Plants don't grow that way in nature, and they shouldn't be replanted around your home that way, either. If you have an almost uncontrollable need to work in straight lines, try this: Once you have determined the general areas where these plants will go, turn your back on the scene and, with a handful of pebbles or colored marbles (easier to spot), toss them over your shoulder. Wherever they land, that's where a plant is placed.

AERATING THE SOIL

After the large items have been planted, it is time to aerate the soil. Heavy feet and heavier equipment have pounded the air pockets out of the soil. This affects the ability of oxygen to penetrate down into the roots and the amount of rainwater the soil can hold.

There was no point in aerating the soil before because the tree spade would have mashed it all down again. Aerate the soil after all heavy equipment has been permanently removed.

There are several acceptable methods for aerating soil. Some people plow and harrow with a small tractor. Some use a garden tiller. Some use a pitchfork and sweat. Motorized lawn aerators can be rented, but they tend to be too shallow. You need to get down at least six inches, and nine is better.

Under a few circumstances this step can be eliminated. If your soil is pure sand with no clay present, it does not get compacted. If all of the topsoil was stored and you built on caliche (sand or clay impregnated with crystalline salts; common in the Southwest) or bedrock, there was no soil to get compacted. Or if you laid down plywood to catch spills and protect the soil, compaction is greatly reduced, although there may still be a few spots where wet conditions and excessive weight caused the soil to harden. If the soil is springy and easy to dig in, it is not compacted. If it is hard to dig in and feels almost like pavement underfoot, it needs aerating.

SPREADING THE SALVAGED TOPSOIL

Remember the topsoil that was scraped off the job site and saved? Now is the time to reintroduce it to the transition zone. Once you have aerated the existing soil, spread the saved soil on top of it. As noted in chapter 5, this topsoil contains seeds, bulbs, roots, and other precious native vegetation. If bulbs, tubers, or sprouting bits of root catch your eye, plant them as you would daffodils or irises where you think they will survive and show to advantage. Shade-loving plants would be placed under a tree or on the north side of the house where they will receive shade. Those that love moisture could be planted next to a drain spout. If you have no idea what the bit of bulb is, plant it where it will get morning sun and afternoon shade, which suits nearly everything. After it has bloomed and you have identified it, you can move it to a better spot if it requires sun or shade all day.

Sometimes the topsoil is lumpy with clumps of clay or caliche subsoil. If you have just a few clumps, break them up with the back of a hoe or soak them in a bucket of water. If you have many lumps, just spread them out and either water the whole area until they "melt" or wait for a good hard rain. Then stay off the soil until it has dried out for a couple of days. Soil with a high clay content will recompact if you walk on it while it is wet. Once the soil has dried to a consistency that is easy to work with, continue planting. Another easy way to let nature break down the clumps is to leave them exposed all winter. Freeze and thaw action will reduce them to crumbles.

PLANTING NEW NATIVE VEGETATION

The majority of your restored plantings will be seeds or the plants that you asked the local nursery to grow for you. You will, most likely, supplement them with other native plants. Do not introduce exotics into this area, particularly high-water-use exotics. If you have old favorites that you love too much to eschew completely, plant them in the patio or entranceway, or in any designated, high-water-use spot that does not affect the integrity of the natural, native landscape.

Nursery-grown plants give you an instant landscape, which is highly satisfying. But in most parts of the country they require diligent watering until they become established—from one to three years. After that, they should be able to make it on their own. Seed gives you a landscape that requires less watering to establish, and the spacing is usually closer to nature's design. Most people use a combination of seeds and plants.

For a true revegetation, all the native seeds would be hand gathered from your lot or from lots in your neighborhood. If you contract with a nursery to grow plants for you, they will do so from seeds you gather, or they will come out and gather seeds and take cuttings from your property.

If you're going to gather the seeds yourself, you'll be doing it from midsummer to early winter. Seeds ripen two weeks to six months after flowering. You will know that the seeds are ready to be harvested when the pods or fruits start to turn from green to tan, yellow, red, or purple—or white fluff. Never strip a plant completely of seed; take no more than 10 percent. In most cases, this can easily be done by gently running your cupped hand down the stem or branch and collecting the ripe seed in your palm. Moist seed should be put in a paper bag and dry seed in a ziplock plastic bag. We often use empty 35-mm film canisters for tiny seeds. If you're collecting more than one kind of seed, keep them separated. If you mistakenly collect some weed and if it is mixed in with the rest, you will just have to throw out all the seed or spend long hours fighting the weed in your landscape.

Don't trust to memory; carry a grease pencil or indelible marker and immediately mark the container, not just with the name of the plant but the kind of habitat in which it was collected—dry hillside or moist low area. Keeping the seeds separated will also help you in planning color schemes and seasonal focal points in your garden. Store the containers in a cool, dark setting: the garage, the fridge, even the freezer. If you notice bugs feasting on the seed, put a snippet of a pet's flea collar into the container.

Cuttings are short lengths of green twigs that can be coaxed into producing roots at one end and leaves at the other to quickly make a new plant. Root cuttings are also an efficient way of producing new plants. If your main ground cover is a thicket shrub or a flower that spreads by root, the nursery could come out just after you have fenced off the envelope and dig mother plants to divide and propagate into dozens of replacement plants. Cuttings produce clones of the original plant, meaning they have exactly the same genes. Seeds produce baby plants with genetic material that reflects both parents.

For the most part, you will be planting around your house precisely the same plant material that was there before you started construction. There are a few exceptions to this rule.

We built on a dry hillside covered with piñon-juniper scrub. The mature understory consisted principally of Gambel oak, lousewort, and rock jasmine Androsace under the trees, and sagebrush, rubber rabbitbrush, mountain mahogany, wild gooseberry, Easter daisy, Santa Fe phlox, bitterweed, scarlet gilia, and two species of buckwheats in the sun. Looking at some of our neighbors' land, we decided that there must have been lots of blue grama, a short grass, knitting this all together before our land had been grazed by sheep and goats.

Our storms come primarily from the northwest, and our house, a two-story, has changed the moisture patterns. On the south, some trees are getting stressed because they are receiving less rain than usual. Here we have to decide whether to water them once a year or let them thin out.

Snow and rain accumulate on the north side of the house, and the roofs drain off in this area, creating a two- to five-foot-wide strip of moist, shady soil. Here we need to plant vegetation that prefers moisture and shade. Plants that have done extremely well are either sunny stream-side flowers or shade-loving ground covers found in a cooler, moister ponderosa woodland up our road at a slightly higher elevation.

MULCHING

Mulch helps hold in moisture. Organic mulches such as compost and decomposing leaves also improve soil permeability and nutrition, all of which make it much easier for roots to obtain food and moisture. In woodlands and prairies, rich, organic soil creates healthy, faster-growing plants. It looks better if you mulch with the same material that creates new soil on your land. For example, if that natural material is a mixture of beech and maple leaves, mulch new plantings with beech and maple leaves. If your natural material is pine needles, mulch with pine needles. You can gather the native mulch you need from your own land. Be careful not to take too much from any one spot because you don't want to rob one area and leave the ground bare. Just take a small amount from various spots.

In our case, the piñon-juniper duff under our undisturbed trees was too thin to share. We have been saving and drying our tea and coffee grounds and broadcasting them under the trees up close to the house. These grounds were the right texture and color to mimic the native mulch, and by the second fall the doctored area looked very natural. By the third spring, a full complement of native shady ground covers suddenly appeared.

Organic mulch is not a natural component of desert soils, so don't add it there. The microorganisms necessary to break it down are not present. In a courtyard garden, you could add a thin layer of decomposed granite, and it looks very nice. However, for your revegetated area, the soil will look best in the long run if you simply allow it and the small rocks in it to reform themselves into desert pavement.

WATERING

In most of the country, large, transplanted trees need to be watered deeply and frequently throughout the first year and into the second year during the summer or whenever the most brutal dry season occurs. The third year, withdraw the support system, and water only if the plants show signs of distress, indicating they are not yet fully reestablished.

Within a year after construction, the transition zone is lush with replanted native vegetations that was either salvaged prior to construction or grown from locally gathered seed. The idea is to create a seamless look from the house out into the natural zone.

The further north you live and the moister the natural soil is, the easier it is to establish plants. In some parts of Canada, one watering on the day you plant is sufficient. In the Southwest, you may have to do fifty waterings the first year, twenty the next, and one or two the third year. That's when it makes sense to put in a temporary drip irrigation system. In those hot, dry climates, it is also often necessary to water the seeds once to get them to germinate and one more time to help the seedlings get established. This is necessary when the weather reports say you are seriously below normal rainfall in spring or fall, when the seeds would normally germinate.

The sooner you can stop supplemental watering, the better. If you water more than necessary, you will produce a vastly different landscape than the one you intended, and your seamless revegetation project will stick out like a sore thumb. It is very hard for people to realize that gardening with nature is easy. They can't really believe that the plants can live without human effort. So look out at your preserved landscape and remind yourself that it was there long before you came along, and it will be most likely be there long after you've gone.

Several years ago, my wife and I had an epi-
phany. Like many Americans, we work out of our home, unfettered by the need to
be in someone else's office between certain set hours. And that meant, we giddily
realized, that we were free to live anywhere we liked. All we needed to continue
earning our humble living was a computer, a phone, and a fax machine. We immediately began speculating on where we wanted to spend the rest of our lives.

Being a native Texan, Sally was drawn to the Hill Country west of Austin. This
rolling countryside is a vibrant riot of wildflowers during much of the year and has
a rugged splendor that we both find very appealing. Unfortunately, our search for a
piece of land led from one dead end to another. All around us, we saw tracts of land
from which native vegetation had been stripped away; natural undulations had
been leveled and all other distinguishing features had been erased and replaced by
conventional lawn-centered landscapes. The beautiful and unique Hill Country
was changed into Anywhere USA!

And then, quite serendipitously, we found what we had been searching for. We
had gone to Taos to share Thanksgiving dinner with an old friend. We had visited
this lovely art and tourist community many times before, but for some inexplicable
reason we had never considered living there. Our friend introduced us to a real es-

Our home, set into the piñon-juniper woodlands outside Taos, New Mexico, is also home to native cowpen daisy, two-year aster, fleabane daisy, golden bromweek, and sagebrush. Wildlife abound here, and so far we've seen jackrabbits, deer, elk, skunks, coyotes, foxes, magpies, scrub jays ... and a bear's paw print!

tate agent, and before we knew what hit us, we found ourselves standing on a heavily wooded piece of land in the foothills thirty minutes north of the picturesque town, gaping at the picture postcard view of Taos Mountain to the southeast. The wintry air was brisk and clean, and redolent with the scent of piñons, junipers, and ponderosa pines. Sally and I looked at each other, grinning like kids who had just inherited a chocolate factory, and simultaneously said yes! It took us all of three seconds to decide to grab it. A year later we began to build on our three-acre tract.

The second, equally important, decision we made that day was to build our home using nature's envelope. We had, after all, been touting it in slide presentations and articles for several years, and if our property didn't deserve this approach, whose did?

OUR ENVELOPE TEAM

For most people, selecting the right architect is a major decision. In chapter 9, I mention how one couple actually interviewed four architects before finding one who not only understood the envelope concept but was enthusiastic about it. We were luckier.

Our architect—Stephen Merdler—was someone I had known since we were kids in New Jersey. But our ties went farther back than that; his mother had actually played matchmaker for my parents in Poland before the war. Having someone we could rely on completely was especially important as we were living in Dallas—a good eleven-and-a-half hour drive away from our property—so we could not pop up for a look at the drop of a hat.

Sally goes over the house plans with our architect, Stephen Merdler, and our builder, Wade Elston. We spent the better part of the day walking the property and deciding where the house would go so as to impact the land as little as possible.

Now living in nearby Santa Fe, Stephen specializes in passive solar energy adobe homes, ranging from moderately priced to way beyond our budget. One reason for his success is that he not only designs environmentally sound homes, but he also designs with a true artist's eye. There's a soft, gentle look to his homes—no sharp edges or hard lines—and a very creative use of space. Years ago, when Sally and I first saw some of his work, we agreed that if we ever lived where the adobe style made sense, Stephen would design our home.

Still, nature's envelope was a relatively new concept for Stephen. He had always attempted to save as much of the natural landscapes on his job sites as he could, but he was often frustrated by clients who preferred to clear away much of the vegetation and "open things up" and by subcontractors who made half-hearted attempts to save a few trees but soon reverted to old habits.

When we explained the steps we intended to take, Stephen immediately tuned in to our plans and produced a knockout design for our adobe hacienda that fit comfortably onto our sloping land. He avoided the prime trees and situated the well, propane tank, and septic system where they would be least disruptive.

One month after first contacting him, we made another trip up to visit our land, and we asked Stephen to meet us there. For the better part of a day we walked the property and marked, with colored ribbons, the trees that must be saved, those that we hoped to save, and those that we begrudgingly admitted would have to go. It was a real "Sophie's Choice" situation, and every time we tagged a tree or shrub for removal we felt like executioners. (We didn't need to hire someone to do a formal plant survey because Sally was fairly well versed in the flora of this part of New Mexico.)

Picking the general contractor was, of course, equally vital to the success of our

Sally marks a tree that must be saved. Other colored ribbons marked vegetation that was dispensable or would be salvaged for transplanting in another spot. This is often a painful "Sophie's choice" kind of exercise, as a number of perfectly healthy and handsome specimens on the construction site would be lost.

plan. The wrong one could undo all our best intentions and, once destroyed, the habitat would be a long time healing. The piñons, while only ten to fifteen feet tall, were from thirty to sixty years old; a few were actually close to a hundred years old.

Stephen warned us that it might be difficult finding a contractor who would do the quality work we wanted and be flexible enough to adopt a new and, for him, radical methodology. Even the best-intentioned builder will be bound by habits acquired over many years of doing it the old way. The average builder believes it is necessary to clear a wide area around the building site.

Here, Stephen really earned his keep. Although he was unfamiliar with Taos builders—his work being mostly in Santa Fe—he prescreened a number of contractors in our area and found several who might fit the bill. The final decision would of course be ours, but we relied heavily on Stephen's expertise and professional instincts. Sally and I were especially gun-shy because, when we were first married, we had hired a contractor to add a second story to our Dallas home. The guy we picked had come recommended by a friend and coworker, and he had a friendly and engaging quality that earned him our trust. That he was the low bidder didn't hurt his case. Boy, were we wrong! This "builder-from-hell" not only wrecked parts of our house that he shouldn't even have been near, he put us six months behind schedule and so far over budget that by the time the work was completed (by another builder—the original guy took down his scaffolding and bolted the scene), we had run through every dime of our savings.

Needless to say, we were determined to be as critical and hard-nosed this time around as our natures permitted. Wade Elston was the one we picked, and we couldn't have made a better decision. Although Wade had never done a home using the envelope, like Stephen he instantly grasped it and in principle liked it. I say "in

Many builders believe it is impossible to work within the confines of the transition zone. As has been proven time and again, it isn't. Scaffolding, for example, only comes out some five feet, allowing subcontractors ample room to maneuver inside the fence.

Materials were stored in the space reserved for guest parking and for the garage. The detached garage was the last structure to be completed.

principle" because at our first meeting he was pretty upfront with his reservations about our "wild idea." For one thing, he thought our five- to fifteen-foot transition zone was unrealistic, although he also admitted that he'd never actually tried doing it our way. During that first meeting, he asked good questions and also made a few suggestions that we'd never thought of. They proved to be good ones.

For example, we knew that we could not save all the trees on the building site. But Wade worked out an excellent deal with a local nursery that saved the best of the junipers and piñons that were in the private zone. The nursery came out with their large tree spade and dug up twenty-five trees, replanted three of them along the road for screening, and took the rest back to the nursery to sell. In this way, the operation didn't cost us a cent. Our builder even invited his son's kindergarten teacher to bring the whole class out to watch—and hopefully to grasp the significance of what we were doing. The kids had a ball while learning an important environmental lesson.

At this same time, we carefully dug up smaller plants—some cacti and yuccas—from the same site and replanted them, although our hopes for their survival were dim. We were doing all this transplanting in the spring—not the ideal time—and a hot and dry summer lay ahead. Wade promised to water the transplants regularly in our absence, but realistically we knew he'd have his hands full coordinating the subcontractors and generally overseeing the job. Watering was not part of his job description, and we didn't want to add one more burden to his workload.

He did the best he could, but that summer turned out to be an especially brutal one. By the time we visited the site in late August, it was clear that we were going to lose the two smaller trees. Amazingly, the large one—twice the size of the others—that we'd placed at the head of our driveway survived.

We also thought we'd lost the yucca we replanted by the road. Yucca has a very deep taproot that is impossible to completely extricate. Even though the one we tried to save was small, we still had to get a good twelve to sixteen inches of root if the plant would have any chance of making it. It looked shriveled and brown by late summer, and we wrote it off. The following spring, Sally was out by the road and suddenly let out a happy whoop! The yucca was making a comeback. Fresh green shoots were showing in the center.

Looking across the transition zone, we can see the proximity of the trees to the house. The fence kept workers out of the natural zone.

The workers were very conscientious about staying out of the natural zone, and we had no real complaints on that score. We never even found a gum wrapper out there. But we did have a problem with some of the pruning they did on several piñons by the fence. Admittedly, these people were not tree surgeons or arborists, so it may be unfair to expect them to know how to prune cosmetically. And we probably should have anticipated it being a greater problem. Early on, Sally had mentioned pruning one or two times, but somehow her admonitions did not come across strongly enough. A few of our trees were pretty well butchered as branches deemed to be too close to the work area were cut back. One juniper, in particular, had all the branches on its house side lopped off because they reached a few feet over the fence. As I mentioned in chapter 5, the branches could have been tied back and saved. Now we'll have to look at this lopsided tree forever.

If we were doing this again, we would instruct the contractor and his key workers on what to do and how to do it. If certain branches were too thick to be tied back and had to be pruned, we would mark where to cut and not leave it up to the inexperienced work crews.

We also feel that we gave in too quickly on another tree that was just a foot and a half away from the northwest wall of the house. It was an eight-foot-tall piñon and had what we called a lot of character. It made a dramatic accent at the corner of the house and early on we had marked it as a definite keeper. But we were persuaded that the stucco would be very difficult, if not impossible, to apply at that point because of the tree's proximity to the wall. As Wade said, "It would be an act of cruelty to the tree." We reluctantly agreed with him but still regret losing the tree. Later we put in a new tree to replace the original, which the builder paid for. But it died despite our best efforts to keep it alive. It's not impossible that, even in this very arid climate, we watered it to death! We tried a juniper next time, which fared much better and is alive and healthy today. But it lacks the charm and personality of the original tree and is only half its size.

We learned that, despite utilizing all the steps in the envelope technique designed to save the trees, the very act of placing a house on a site has to affect their well-being to some degree. As mentioned in chapter 5, the structure can cause a "rain shadow" that blocks rain and snow-melt runoff. The structure also covers up far-spreading surface roots, reducing the water supply. If extensive excavation is needed, as for a cellar, that too can seriously harm the root system. A fence around the perimeter just isn't going to shield the trees from all possible harm.

This seems so obvious today, but it honestly never occurred to us when we began construction. Now we know that we should have irrigated our threatened trees for at least the first summer, and possibly the second as well, to help them regrow their root systems and recover from the stress of construction. Because we

Workers' cars and trucks carried the seeds of numerous weeds to our site.

And since weeds love disturbed areas such as construction sites, we were faced with having to dig them up or spray them with glysophate.

had never expected to water the natural zone, it being so well established, we did not install water faucets on the outside walls—a big mistake.

During our first spring, we realized that we had an infestation of weeds along the dirt road by our home. Yellow sweet clover, tumbleweed, burs, and other noxious invaders appeared in great numbers, and we had to spend several afternoons pulling and bagging them. By the second spring, we resorted to spraying glysophate (commonly marketed as Roundup™ and other commercial herbicides) because the task of eliminating them by hand was actually perpetuating the problem; each time we pulled a weed, we disturbed the soil and created the very environment that favored weeds over natives.

Was this infestation going to be an annual event? Why hadn't we noticed all these weeds before we started building? The answer was that there hadn't been very many, and the ones that we had seen were not along our property line. What we did notice was that everywhere someone had built, or where a road had been cut into the woods, weeds sprang up. Weeds love disturbed areas, and many of them arrived because the workers unintentionally carried the seeds up to the site on the tires and bumpers of their vehicles. Everywhere they had parked along the road was suddenly lush with noxious knapweed, thistle, and more!

We wondered if a local ordinance could be enacted to mandate municipal road graders, telephone company trucks, and other such vehicles to be hosed down before driving into a natural area. But we realized that this would be difficult to enforce and would be impossible with regard to the private cars of construction workers. Rosa Finsley, a landscape architect and friend in Dallas, has solved this problem by laying down sheets of plywood to make a safe parking area.

WHAT OUR BUILDER LEARNED

Two and a half years after our home was completed, Wade told me (yes, we're still on speaking terms) that while he has not had another pure envelope job since ours, the experience has influenced his thinking on other jobs. He continues to use fencing to protect key vegetation on job sites. He does it on his own, and not at the homeowners' request. Because he had to work around our house within the fifteen-foot-wide transition zone, he realized that he could accomplish what needed to be done without heavy equipment. Many of the supplies that would ordinarily have been driven to where they were needed were hand-carried instead. A little more labor and time, but a lot less impact on the site. Today, the biggest earthmover he brings onto a job site is a backhoe. "It's less heavy-handed," he said, "more surgical."

He also said he installed the septic system much earlier than he normally would have, not being able to move the tank into place through what became the natural zone. It had to be installed before the fence went up and the foundation laid.

The one exception to the "no entering" rule imposed on the natural zone was one we couldn't argue with. Wade set up lawn sprinklers outside the fence and made sure the trees were regularly irrigated. H did this on his own initiative, and for two reasons: first, we were building our home during one of northern New Mexico's driest periods in many years. Second, he was aware that the construction activities would stress the trees, and he was as concerned about their survival as we were. This was just one more confirmation that we had made the right choice.

SPREADING THE WORD

About a year before we began building, we received a phone call from the people who had just purchased the lot next door. They wanted to know if we would be interested in a well-share. This is fairly common in these parts, wells being a major

Freshly fallen snow emphasizes our close proximity to the forest.

expense. We agreed for two reasons: it cut that expense in half, and it meant that there would be less impact on the land. Sally and I had witnessed one well going in down the road. Several trees had been knocked down in the process, and the ground was pretty badly torn up when the equipment was moved into place.

As we got to know our neighbors-to-be, we discussed with them our intention to build using nature's envelope. They immediately liked the concept, asked me for details, and ultimately used the technique for their home. Their builder shared some of Wade's reservations, but successfully tucked their home into the woods with a minimum of impact on the property.

Later, the *Taos News* ran an article on how we were building our home. Consequently, we received an invitation to address the local realtors at one of their luncheon meetings. The response was very positive, and I can only hope that they will introduce the envelope to customers buying natural properties.

✠ Green
Developments ✠ 8

When Joseph Hooker, a renowned nine-teenth-century biologist and friend of Charles Darwin, addressed the British Scientific Society in 1866 on the biology of islands, he told his audience that islands are at risk because they are small and isolated. Today, almost all of our natural habitats are fragmented and environmentally dysfunctional landscapes—not unlike islands—the result of car-oriented, lawn-centered real estate development. Hooker's warning is still relevant.

The envelope concept, of course, is a response to these fragmented landscapes. When a developer undertakes to create an entire community using this technique, this has come to be called a "green development." It is as unlike a traditional subdivision as a five-course banquet is unlike a fast-food lunch. Jim Hill, of the federal government's Green Building Council, points out that a healthier ecology is a primary long-term benefit of green developments.

From coast to coast we are seeing a growing number of green developments, both residential and commercial. In this chapter we describe some notable examples.

DEWEES ISLAND, SOUTH CAROLINA

There are two things you won't find at Dewees Island: cars and lawns. You arrive at this beautiful 1,206-acre barrier island by ferry, a fifteen-minute ride. When

The only way to reach Dewees Island, off the coast of South Carolina, is by ferry. Transportation within the community is by golf cart.

A home on Dewees Island nestled into the coastal vegetation.

you get there, transportation is provided by a fleet of battery-powered golf carts. According to the development's subdivision policy, "Formal lawns are not allowed. Landscape plants must be native to the coastal plain barrier island."

John L. Knott Jr., the guiding force behind Dewees Island, turns to nature to explain the concept of green development and this island community. "A bird," he says, "does not tear down the tree to live in it; she builds a nest that becomes a part of the tree. The ant does not poison the soil to make its home; it builds a nest that becomes a part of the soil. Only humans construct homes that are at odds with their ecosystem. Such a course of conduct is shortsighted, both ecologically and economically."

Located twelve miles northeast of Charleston, South Carolina, Dewees Island was begun in 1991. The master plan called for more than 65 percent of the island to be protected from any development, and 350 acres on the northeastern end of the island have been designated as a wildlife refuge. The development also employs a full-time environmental programs coordinator and a full-time landscape ecologist.

The developer's reverence for the island is reflected in one of the sales brochures: "Brown flats of oysters, here long before man, lined her banks, and fireflies had illuminated her silky blackness through billions of nights. She had served as a rest stop for dozens of varieties of migrating ducks, and has seen the rise and fall of the tide for over 500 centuries."

Thus, before a single home was built, an environmental consultant worked with the state's Department of Natural Resources to prepare a comprehensive wildlife management plan. Builder education was another major reason for the success of this venture; all builders were required to attend seminars so they could learn about the environment and how to protect it. The infrastructure—roads, composting systems, telephone, power, waste treatment, marina, boardwalks, and a reverse osmosis water treatment system—was designed to minimize the impact on the natural ecosystem.

The 150 home sites were selected on the basis of careful analysis of the soils, topography, wetlands, and plants and animal life. The buildings are designed to take full advantage of natural heating, cooling, and lighting.

Knott created Dewees Island based on his belief that "we simply need to rediscover our intuitive base about how to live in harmony with our environment, as opposed to dominating and destroying more than we need." This approach, which he formulated into seven guiding principles, has resulted not only in ecological benefits but also in economic benefits—to property owners, to the developer, and to the community as a whole. These principles are:

* Development and environment are natural allies.
* All development should occur in the context that all resources are limited.
* Communities can be resource providers, not just resource users.
* Land is a stewardship role for future generations.
* It is less expensive, in the short and long term, to build in harmony with the environment.
* Communities are planned for people, and technologies are to be supportive, not dominant.
* Environmental education is an essential first step in the rediscovery of our intuitive sense of integrating with the environment.

The success of Dewees Island is evidenced by the fact that each year some three thousand building professionals visit this community to learn and find inspiration.

Sea Ranch
(above and right)

Anyone who has ever driven along the northern coastline of California has been moved by the magnificent beauty of this terrain. On one side is the Pacific Ocean, crashing against the rocks below, and on the other the rugged foothills rising into dense woodlands.

Sea Ranch had its genesis in 1963 when Alfred Boeke, an architect and a land planner, advised Oceanic California, Inc., to purchase 5,000 acres of this majestic land north of San Francisco. He envisioned a community built on respect for the natural landscape in all its variations: coastline, meadows, uplands, and forests. As described by Richard Sexton in his book *Parallel Utopias*, "Sea Ranch is a community inspired by the idealized country life. It is a development pattern that accommodates relatively large numbers of people (over twenty-three hundred homesites on about four thousand acres), but maintains the natural environment as the dominant impression."

As the principal charged with overseeing the project, Boeke hired San Francisco–based architect Lawrence Halprin to design the first 1,800 acres marked for development. Halprin broke with tradition and chose to leave the coastal bluffs undeveloped. Conventional thinking at that time held that this was the most desirable land, offering the best views of the ocean, and was therefore more valuable. But he realized that if these coastal meadows and bluffs were kept open, they would be enjoyed by all.

Halprin described Sea Ranch as "antisuburban" because it has very little "vest-pocket nature in it." By this he meant formal landscaped gardens. While gardens and landscaped areas containing exotic plants are permitted, they are confined to private homes and are in courtyard areas or behind board fences, preserving the public view of the natural terrain.

The natural environment is further protected by a number of documents called The Sea Ranch Restrictions: A Declaration of Restrictions, Covenants and Conditions, which functions as the community's constitution. Another document, the Design Committee Rules, establishes guidelines for development and ensures that human activities will have minimal impact on the land.

Homes are constructed according to strict architectural guidelines that promote their assimilation into the natural landscape. For the most part, natural siding is used and the houses are painted in pale earth tones that blend unobtrusively into the coastal landscape.

Half of the acreage at Sea Ranch is designated as common area and is open to residents for hiking, wildlife watching, and recreation. Sea lions can be spotted sunning on the rocks, while deer, rabbits, and many other woodland creatures roam the land.

Historically, this land had been logged and then grazed, leaving little in the way of true indigenous vegetation. The land recovered over the years with the help of a state initiative limiting development density and setting aside more of the coastline as natural areas. Also, while 2,000 acres were left undeveloped, several parcels were designated "timber production areas," with the proviso that no clear cutting would be permitted. Only minimal, selective cutting would occur.

Initially, three coastal native pines—Bishop pine *Pinus muricata*, shore pine *P. contorta*, and Monterey pine *P. radiata*—were planted. The land has been permitted to heal itself; today it is predominantly native vegetation, and the grasslands are now beginning a natural succession to forest. According to Bill Wiemeyer, environmental planner at Sea Ranch, controlled burning is now being introduced to maintain these grasslands, although dubious homeowners had to be educated to the benefits of this proven method of land management.

PORTOLA VALLEY RANCH, CALIFORNIA

In 1983, Nancy Hardesty, who was involved in Portola Valley Ranch as a landscape architect, wrote that "California is its sturdy and enduring oaks. The Heritage Oaks of today were seedlings when the Pilgrims established the Plymouth Colony in 1620. These same oaks were awkward youngsters 150 years old when the Declaration of Independence was signed in 1776. Today, these same trees are ancient, wide-spreading sculptural silhouettes on the California skyline. Young, new oaks have been suppressed and destroyed by man and his animals. We must restore the oak woodlands and protectively escort these valuable native trees into California's twenty-first century."

It was these majestic oaks of northern California that no doubt first attracted settlers to this region. It was certainly what brought developer Joseph Whelan to these gently rolling hills, grassy open spaces, and venerable woodlands located midway between San Francisco and San Jose, and led him to purchase the 450-acre site in the early 1970s.

His intention was to create a residential development, and the following year he approached the town of Portola Valley with his plans. Although environmentally oriented developers often complain about municipalities being a source of frustrating building codes that tie their hands, Whelan discovered a refreshingly different attitude in this community. Under the leadership of town planner George Mader and local naturalist Herbert J. Dengler, this progressive community had already laid down firm guidelines designed to protect the area's unique beauty and ecosystem.

While Whelan's project was encouraged, no construction began until an exhaustive environmental study was carried out. This study involved a team of landscape architects, land planners, architects, attorneys, economists, geologists, engineers, and naturalists, as well as input from the California Native Plant Society. In the preface to this study, Whelan wrote, "Over the centuries Nature formed this land and selected appropriate adornments. We do not presume to improve upon her choices."

Portola Valley Ranch

One vital aspect of this work involved an extensive seismic study, since the development site was bisected by an earthquake fault. A geology map was developed to assure that cul-de-sacs would be situated away from potential landslide areas and homes would be built only on firm bedrock. In addition, a detailed land management report was created that covered everything from control of invasive plant species to landscape irrigation guidelines to proper care of the native oaks and grasslands.

This community of 205 single-family homes clustered on approximately 100 acres with a 350-acre open space of unspoiled oak woodlands later received the prestigious 1984 ASLA Award. The design philosophy of Portola Valley Ranch integrates all humanly made elements into small cul-de-sacs, which are situated below ridge lines. Roads connecting the residential clusters follow the ridge lines, for minimal disturbance to the topography. These clusters are further connected by rustic footpaths to the seven-acre community recreation center and feed into a ten-mile network of hiking, jogging, and riding trails that wind throughout the property.

Marilyn Walter, who served on the town conservation committee and handled marketing for Portola Valley Ranch, said that "the success of this community is due largely to the close and supportive relationship between the developer and the town planners. When Joseph Whelan first approached us, he probably didn't realize how seriously we take land conservation. But he certainly became a convert to the concept."

DESERT HIGHLANDS, ARIZONA

One of the most fragile environments is desert. This was driven home to me about ten years ago as I was walking through a stretch of southwestern desert with a friend. Suddenly, he stopped and pointed to an obviously disturbed spot. "That was an Indian encampment," he said, "about a hundred and fifty years ago. The signs are still here. The land has not yet fully recovered."

Envelope home under Pinnacle Peak

Nonnative plants, such as this tropical bougainvillea, are permitted at Desert Highlands, but only next to the home or in interior patio areas, where they can receive extra watering. The integrity of the natural and transition zones is maintained.

Gage Davis—who wears three professional hats: architect, landscape architect, and urban planner—understands this very well. In 1981, he was commissioned to design and oversee development of Desert Highlands, an 850-acre residential community in North Scottsdale, Arizona. And because of this fragility, he understood immediately that Desert Highlands would be an especially good environment to prove the effectiveness of nature's envelope.

Located at the base of picturesque Pinnacle Peak Mountain, the land Desert Highlands occupies is a prime example of the ruggedly beautiful Sonoran Desert. The topography consists of ravines, washes, dramatic rock outcroppings, and fields of boulders. It is also alive with a wide variety of wildlife: desert tortoises, colorful chuckwalla lizards, roadrunners, and hummingbirds galore, as well as a vast palette of indigenous flora, from armies of stately saguaros and luminescent backlit chollas and ocotillos, to the softer, gentler shapes of palo verde, creosote, fairyduster, bur sage, and brittlebush.

Davis's goal was a subtle blending of people, structures, and desert habitat into a harmonious and aesthetically pleasing community.

At Desert Highlands, undisturbed desert is the unifying theme, and nature's envelope has been formalized as a part of the purchase agreement, which sets down specific guidelines for both landscaping and home design. In fact, it is mandatory that property owners or their architects, builders, or representatives meet with the community's design review committee to discuss proposed plans and resolve any questions that exist about building here.

"But no one who lives here," says Davis, "feels unfairly restricted. In fact, great creativity in home designs—in materials and styles—is evident throughout the community. I know of a number of residents who were attracted to Desert Highlands because of our envelope philosophy. They agree with us that property owners should be stewards of the land and its resources."

Design workshops are conducted for owners who are interested in learning more about the Sonoran landscape and how to design homes that fit into it harmoniously. While high water use exotics are allowed in the private zones, they must not intrude on the overall integrity of the land. A tall Italian poplar, for example, would not be permitted, since it would tower over the house and be visually jarring.

Davis is enthusiastic about the future of the envelope and predicts that it will catch on all over the country, especially in areas where natural habitats are particularly vulnerable. His own company is currently using this technique at projects in Washington, Oregon, Colorado, and Texas.

SEASIDE, FLORIDA

This picturesque self-contained community on the Florida shore of the Gulf of Mexico was designed to reflect the finest ideals of small-town America. Seaside combines homes, shops, businesses, schools, and parks within easy walking distance. It qualifies as a green development because, in 1982, when founder Robert S. Davis met with Douglas Duany, Seaside's landscape architect, Duany asked Davis how he envisioned the landscaping. Davis pointed toward the windswept scrub and the sugary white sands and said, "I sort of like what's out there now."

No local nurseries were then carrying the sand live oak, woody goldenrod, bluestem grass, and wild lupins that constitute the local scrub forests. Davis later said that one of his contractors "almost took my head off when I told him he couldn't simply scrape the lot with a bulldozer and fix it later with grass and shrubs."

When I visited Seaside a few years ago, I had a strange sense of unreality. Just a week earlier my wife and I had seen the Jim Carrey movie *The Truman Show*, which had been filmed here. I half-expected the rubber-faced comedian to come strolling down the sidewalk toward me, a mile-wide grin on his face.

Interestingly, when the film was shot here, Carrey's movie residence had to have a lawn, it being a stereotypical American home, and so the natural vegetation had to be torn up and replaced with Kentucky bluegrass sod. Once the shooting was over, however, the grass was banished and the original vegetation was replaced. Lawns are verboten in Seaside, and only native species or plants from an approved list are permitted in the front yards. Garden writer Michael Pollan, having spent a few days at Seaside, reflected that he "had a vision of what post-lawn America might look like."

Pollan is not the only media person to "discover" Seaside. *Travel & Leisure* magazine said that "it contains the seed of a land-development philosophy that

Seaside

could influence the way America lives in the 21st century," while *Time* magazine called it "the most astounding design achievement of its era, and one might hope, the most influential." It has also been featured in *USA Today*, and on the *Today Show*, *This Old House*, *NBC Nightly News*, *CNN*, *20/20*, and Canadian television. Its collection of architectural awards is long and impressive. The community was even noted by British royalty. Prince Charles said that "I believe that the lessons they're working out at Seaside have very serious applications, both in rural areas and in our cities."

Designed by architects Andres Duany and Elizabeth Plater-Zyberk, Seaside is an eighty-acre unincorporated community fronting on a half-mile of beach.

Although it is not by any stretch of the imagination a typical beachfront development, perhaps its most outstanding feature is its landscaping—lush thickets of native plants including live oak, Southern magnolia, and beach rosemary, to name a few. But, as Pollan noted, the most revolutionary aspect of the place is its willingness "to abolish something as fundamental as the American front lawn."

Randy Harelson, owner of the Garden Gourd, a native plant nursery two miles east of Seaside, and a consultant with Seaside's town council on horticultural matters, says that while the landscape may get little credit for Seaside's notoriety, "if you try looking at the architecture by itself, mentally removing the scrub and replacing it with lawn and foundation plantings, it gets boring very quickly."

Homeowner acceptance of the native landscaping was born out a few years ago when city planners proposed removing the native scrub vegetation on the median strip of Seaside Avenue, the town's main drag, and replacing it with manicured turf grass. The resulting outcry from residents soon changed their minds.

THE WOODLANDS

Begun in 1974, making it one of the earliest green developments in the country, The Woodlands is a 25,000-acre incorporated residential community twenty-seven miles north of downtown Houston, Texas. It was the vision of developer George P. Mitchell and was conceived as a self-sustaining "real hometown" in which residents could live, work, play, and interact on many levels. In addition to over 15,000 occupied homes, the community includes some 600 companies employing over 13,000 people, as well as a hospital, a performing arts pavilion, and an executive conference center.

Beyond that, the aim, as stated in the residents' guide, is "to live in harmony with nature." Homes are tucked back among the loblolly pines and live oaks, sweet

The Woodlands

Maintaining the natural look of the community, commercial zones are screened from the major arteries, with only discreet signs indicating what lies beyond the trees.

gums, and red maples, and even commercial areas—shops, gas stations, and fast food outlets—are discreetly screened by canopy and understory trees.

To achieve his vision, Mitchell hired Ian McHarg to develop the environmental plan for this new community. McHarg, an internationally known and respected ecologist, and the author of *Design with Nature*, dedicated his life to changing the way we see humanity's role in relation to the natural world. Never shy about speaking his mind, McHarg has been quoted as saying that conventional development is "the ransacking of the world's last great cornucopia." He called his hometown of Glasgow, Scotland, "a memorial to an inordinate capacity to create ugliness."

When he returned to The Woodlands to celebrate the community's tenth anniversary, he pronounced it an "exemplary development." He further said that "the development of The Woodlands is important because it demonstrates that you can, in fact, create a livable community while being sensitive to the environment and while making a very profitable enterprise."

McHarg believed that, once exposed to this kind of environment, residents would have their expectations raised and would demand the same kind of ecological considerations at the next place they or their children live.

Residents receive guidelines on landscaping, including detailed plant lists describing the vegetation and growth habits. Unfortunately, all this information is presented as suggestions, and the envelope philosophy was never made a part of the residents' covenants. As a result, many of the homeowners have strayed from the initial concept.

"The people like being surrounded by the forest," observes Wanda Jones, a landscape designer who lives and works in The Woodlands, "but over the years, many have brought in their own landscapers, who cut down most of the trees right around their homes and put in clipped hedges, exotic plants and lawns—a more conventional look." Today, with natural landscaping growing in popularity, Wanda's company, Nature's Touch, is busy turning many of those conventional landscapes back into natural ones.

Nature's envelope is not limited to large-scale developments way out in the "boonies." Often individual homeowners, such as the Cyriers whom we met in the introduction, decide on their own to preserve the natural beauty and character of their lots. Sometimes these envelopes are located right in the middle of developed suburban neighborhoods, on lots that developers or builders hadn't gotten to yet. Sometimes, these lots are sandwiched in between conventionally landscaped homes.

One such envelope home is in Arlington, Texas, a heavily populated bedroom community mid-way between Dallas and Fort Worth. Built by Cindy Hollar and Kevin Tennison, the modern 2,100-square-foot home is on a three-quarter acre lot at one end of a cul-de-sac and is dense with elms, post oaks, redbuds, rusty blackhaw viburnum, roughleaf dogwoods, and coralberries. Naturally, the couple was reluctant to disturb the lot's natural beauty. In fact, the land had a lot of personal history for Cindy; it is three houses away from her childhood home and where her mother, landscape designer Molly Hollar, still lives. "I played there as a kid," she says, "and I'd had my eye on it as a homesite for years."

Although the other lots in the cul-de-sac had been developed with conventional lawn-centered landscapes, this lot remained untouched. It had been owned by a pri-

Flanked by typical suburban homes, the Hollar-Tennison home cannot be seen from the street. It is tucked into this woodland and only the mailbox gives it away.

The living room view is spectacular, showing the seasonal changes of the woodland and the comings and goings of the many species of wildlife that thrive here.

vate party who had long planned on building there himself. But in 1994 Cindy and Kevin convinced him that the lot really had their name on it.

"After we bought the property," Cindy recalls, "I recall standing on the land with my mother, looking at all that beautiful vegetation and saying that I hated losing it. My mother said that I didn't have to, and we made plans to build our house in a way that would preserve most of those trees and understory."

Cindy and Kevin interviewed four architects before finding Ray Schaumberg, who immediately understood the concept and what they wanted. Picking the contractor was easier; Dan Driscoll, a friend of Kevin's, was enthusiastic about the concept from the beginning. "We didn't put a fence around the trees," Cindy says, "but Dan was very vigilant and protective. Both Dan and I had a lot of personal contact with all the subcontractors, and we explained exactly what we had in mind and what we expected. The workers were very respectful of the plan, and they really got into it. On their own initiative, they roped back a redbud that was standing where they were applying stucco and saved the tree." Cindy reflected that it certainly hadn't hurt their cause when they dropped off a few cases of beer for the workers.

Cindy and Kevin were lucky in their choice of subcontractors and also in the fact that the lot had a naturally bare area to one side where equipment and supplies were stored. When the home was completed, they calculated that it had not cost them any more to build with the envelope than if they'd scraped the lot.

When I visited their newly completed home to take pictures, one of their neighbors came outside and told me, wistfully, that she would have loved having a similar landscape—had she only known it was possible.

The home that Mary and Dick Stanley built on two and a half acres of woodland in Dellwood, Minnesota, demonstrates how to incorporate specific features of the property into the overall design. For example, a pond and wetland are situated at one side of the land where sensitive fern, water lilies, arrowheads, and blue flag irises flourish. With normal construction methods, this priceless feature might have been filled in and destroyed.

The project, which ran from 1988 to 1989, was described by their architect, Walter Johanson, as a team effort. "The Stanleys, the contractor, and I had a won-

The Minnesota home of Mary and Dick Stanley sits on two and a half acres of native woodland consisting of numerous indigenous shade and understory trees, including red oaks, white oaks, red maples, pin cherries, aspens, basswoods, and dogwoods.

The view from the enclosed porch delivers a year-round visual delight. The Stanleys said that the only barrier they used to protect the natural zone was a length of rope, but that all the subcontractors understood what they were doing and were very cooperative.

derful rapport in working out all the details of the job." Johanson, whose previous experience lay primarily in designing commercial buildings, had never done an envelope home before, but his style and temperament were well-known to the builder, Phil Anderson, who recommended him to the Stanleys. Anderson-Sorenson Construction, on the other hand, had done a number of envelope homes before the Stanley job.

Both Anderson and Johanson agree that the main reason the home turned out to be what Anderson called "a classic example of the envelope" was the Stanleys themselves, especially Mary, who had a major hand in planning both the home and the preservation of the landscape.

Mary, a nature lover, made certain that a number of trees, which might have been cut down to make room for a deck or walkway, were instead retained, and the structures were creatively designed to literally embrace these trees. A fish pond that occupied a corner of their lot was so close to the building site that it might easily have been filled in and lost had not everyone involved been so scrupulous about preserving as much as they could.

Early on it was decided to delay building the garage until the house itself was completed. This gave the construction team ample room for the storage of materials and equipment, as well as easy access to the building site. Instead of fencing to protect the natural area, ropes were strung up around the site. This proved adequate because, as Mary says, "the workers understood what we were doing and were very conscientious about protecting the landscape." She recalls that she ventured beyond the ropes one day to transplant some wildflowers, and a carpenter working on the roof, spotted her. "Hey, lady," he yelled, a big grin on his face, "you're not supposed to be in there!"

Sometimes a little creative thinking can save vegetation that would ordinarily be cut down. Here a tree is incorporated into the deck, providing shade for the Stanleys and additional habitat for songbirds.

When asked about the future of the envelope, Phil Anderson remarked that it would be a difficult concept for many builders to adopt. "A lot of contractors will steer away from it if they can. The envelope requires more front-end planning, and that's a hard period to get compensated for," he says. "They want to get in, do the job, and clear out. Most builders feel that they don't get paid till the machinery shows up."

Moreover, he says, it can be a hard sell to the average property owner. "It's a question of personal values. People tend to put their money into the house itself. If it's a choice between saving a tree and putting in a bay window, the bay window usually wins."

Still, he and his partner are enthusiastic about the technique and continue to encourage property owners to utilize it whenever possible.

When John Gutting's home was profiled in a 1987 issue of *Mid-Atlantic Country* magazine, the writer, Egon Weck, thought that it was a perfect fit with its natural surroundings. He described it as looking as if it had been "pushed up through the ground by a force of nature."

A landscape architect, Gutting had always wanted to live in the midst of nature, without a square inch of lawn on the property, and in 1980 he set about to make that dream come true.

Initially he and his family lived in the suburban community of Wye. But that was going to be temporary. Gutting spent many weekends touring the countryside with real estate agents searching for his ideal natural setting. He finally found it in Church Hill on the Delmarva Peninsula, at the end of a half-mile gravel road. It

Situated in a seventy-acre tract of woodland on Maryland's eastern shore, John Gutting's home is the culmination of a long-held dream—owning a home in the wilderness.

took four days for him to walk the property and survey the native flora, and only then did he decide to purchase it.

"My objective was to find a natural site and preserve as much of it as possible," he says. It was certainly worth preserving. The native canopy is composed of red and silver maples and a wide variety of hickories, ashes, and oaks. The understory trees include downy serviceberry, eastern redbud, common persimmon, sweetbay magnolia, and blackhaw, while the ferns, vines, shrubs, and woodland wildflowers are far too numerous to list here. As Gutting puts it, "They define this spot."

Finding the right architect was not a problem; Gutting designed the home himself. And he did most of the construction with his own hands. The home itself is glass and wood and is intended to be an unobtrusive addition to the landscape. Gutting's ingenious use of interior space, as well as the way the home is nestled into the woodland setting, earned him *Mid-Atlantic Country*'s 1987 Heritage Award for new home architecture and design.

Gutting divided the property into four fifteen- to eighteen-acre tracts, selling three to friends and keeping the prime location, where several high knolls look down on a fifteen-foot-wide stream, for himself and his family. Some might have built atop the knolls, but Gutting felt that this place of unique beauty should be left unspoiled and located his home elsewhere. To protect the rest of the land, he had a land utilization plan drawn up to ensure that his future neighbors would also respect the integrity of the land. Nonnative species are restricted from the property, and only judicious selective pruning and cutting is allowed.

In addition, when Gutting purchased the land, it became a wildlife sanctuary; all hunting was prohibited, and creatures that once were scarce, such as flying squirrels, are now seen in abundant numbers.

The home of landscape architect Johnny Mayronne in Covington, Louisiana, is surrounded by woodlands and a wetland. With rare exceptions, all the vegetation on the property is native.

There is virtually no original prairie left in this country, so homeowners in the Midwest who want to live in a prairie setting most often have to re-create this habitat. The home of Dave and Roselee Wondra in Chanhassen, Minnesota, was originally an alfalfa field but now displays numerous species of grasses and forbs. In fact, it was so attractive that Dave had no trouble talking his next-door neighbors into converting their two acres into prairie as well.

Gutting is not merely concerned with the preservation of his own property but also focuses on the entire planet. "Over the past 10,000 years," he says, "we humans have increasingly destroyed a place here or there, but we now are working at a global scale. We have to immediately pay attention to the Earth's dictates for all its inhabitants or our remaining stay will become shorter and harsher." Salvation, he concludes, must come not just from controlling our population growth but reversing the trend. "By the year 2100," he says, "there needs to be 50 percent less of us and 100 percent more wilderness."

Recycling is not new. Back in the 1960s, I visited Rhyolite, an old ghost town in Death Valley, California, that had its heyday back around 1890. One of the buildings still standing at that time was, incredibly, a house made from thousands of beer bottles. Apparently conventional building supplies were very expensive and in short supply in this remote desert setting. But the town's numerous saloons provided an endless supply of empty beer bottles, and they were free for the taking.

Today, using unconventional building materials, as well as exploring unconventional techniques, is becoming, well, more conventional. Called green building, this concept is closely allied with green developments and the envelope, and it is gaining popularity as developers realize that more aesthetically pleasing, environmentally sound, and cost-effective alternatives to traditional building methods exist. Green building is carried on in Canada by the R-2000 Program, in Texas by the Green Builders Program in Austin, in New Mexico by the Star Homes program in Santa Fe. It is an important part of the educational programming offered by the National Association of Home Builders. Even former Soviet leaders are getting into the act: Mikhail Gorbachev now sits on the board of directors of Global Green USA, an organization dedicated to, among other things, promoting a sustainable balance between the environment and development.

Green building involves exploring and utilizing more environmentally friendly building materials such as recycled metal framing instead of wood, recycled plastic soda bottles that are converted into carpeting, and chopped-up styrofoam coffee cups from McDonald's that are transformed into building blocks. Homes are no longer set down just anywhere; their relation to the sun is taken into consideration to give them the benefits of passive solar energy. Homes achieve greater energy efficiency with walls constructed out of straw bales, adode, bamboo, and even corn cobs.

When I first became interested in tracking down examples of nature's envelope, I was living in Dallas, Texas, and the first ones I found were relatively close to home. One of the first people I met was Larry Peel, a developer in Austin. Peel utilizes nature's envelope in the construction of his condominium and townhouse communities, and he finds that the results are very marketable.

At his Park Mesa Condominiums, residents not only appreciate the beauty of the native vegetation that surrounds their units, but they like the privacy screening provided by thickets of Ashe junipers. The slopes below the condominiums are colorful with Englemann daisies, which are allowed to grow unmowed, and the red berries of evergreen sumac. At another of his properties, Stillhouse Condominiums, Peel provided screening between the parking lots and the units, so residents can look out at trees and flowers and birds instead of cars and boat trailers. On all of his construction sites, Peel uses orange plastic fencing to mark off the natural areas.

When corporations began moving their headquarters from downtown office buildings to suburban locales, they copied the conventional landscaping techniques of their homeowner neighbors—lawn-centered expanses with exotic flower beds around the entrances and driveways. But in recent years, a few innovative compa-

Park Mesa Condominiums in Austin, Texas

At Stillhouse Condominiums, developer Larry Peel preserved these native trees to provide natural screening between the buildings and the parking lot.

nies have begun to see "green" as more than an annual report objective, and they have placed their buildings in more natural surroundings.

Mike Cuhady, CEO of Marquette Electronics (now GE Marquette Medical Systems) in Milwaukee, Wisconsin, had something very specific in mind for his seventy-five-acre white oak woodland. He wanted a peaceful, contemplative place for his engineers—a creative environment that was free from the daily pressures and problems of working at the main plant. His woodland, the last natural area remaining within the city limits, was ideal.

The Marquette Electronics research facility was built in these woodlands within the city limits of Milwaukee. The setting was so peaceful that the owner, Mike Cudahy, moved his own office out there—to "crack the whip."

From the beginning, Cudahy found resistance from his contractor, who wanted to clear a minimum of 100 feet around the facility's footprint. "Impossible," barked Cudahy. "Well, how much *can* I clear?" asked the contractor. "No more than twenty feet," Cudahy responded. "Impossible," replied the contractor. "Not impossible," said Cudahy. "If they can build skyscrapers in New York City just a half-inch from the skyscraper next door, then you can build inside the twenty-foot limit!"

Cudahy got his woodland sanctuary. But, according to James McClintock, his architect, "He was almost too successful. The engineers loved the new woodland facility so much that they spent too much time staring out the windows looking at the deer." Cudahy wound up moving his own office out there, "to crack the whip."

One major disappointment concerned a majestic 200-year-old oak situated at entrance to the facility. Cudahy envisioned it at the center of the circular driveway. But tree experts brought in to evaluate the flora on the property told him the tree posed a danger. They told Cudahy that the oak was rotten to the core and would topple over onto the new building. Reluctantly, he agreed to having the tree cut down. "After it had been felled," he says, sadly, "we could see that it had been perfectly sound."

The research facility occupies twenty acres of the property; the remaining fifty-five acres is family homestead, including a 6,500-square-foot house built in 1926. The house was too grand to tear down, so Cudahy resolved to move it. At first, he had planned to cut it into three sections and cart it off on wide-bed trailers. But this would have required taking down far too many trees to make room for the large loads. He then considered hoisting the house out with Sikorsky helicopters, but that too threatened the woodland. Finally, he had the entire house dismantled, piece by piece, and trucked off to its new location. Cudahy then donated the fifty-five-acre property to the YMCA for a performing and visual arts center. The preserved woodland is a dramatic setting for this new edifice.

One of the most impressive envelope campuses is found in Atlanta, Georgia, home of the world headquarters of United Parcel Service (UPS). Situated on thirty-six acres of oak woodlands, UPS turned to Spence Rosenfeld to help develop the site. Rosenfeld, founder and president of Arborguard Tree Specialists in Avondale Estates, Georgia, holds a master's degree in urban forestry from Duke University and is a nationally recognized leader in arborculture and conservation work.

If conventional means had been employed in the construction of UPS's 620,000-square-foot headquarters, much of the site's native ecosystem would have been lost. Instead, more than two-thirds of the acreage was left untouched. A single access road was built and materials were stored off-site. Areas that were disturbed during the building phase were revegetated with 900 native oaks *Quercus* spp., flowering dogwood *Cornus florida*, and magnolias *Magnolia* spp.

Woodland wildlife is abundant on the grounds and a mile-long nature trail is used by both local residents and employees. There is also an outdoor dining area adjacent to the company cafeteria that encourages enjoyment of the natural setting. "The entire work setting," says UPS employee Susan Rosenberg, "from the native landscape to the building design that includes large windows, allows employees to incorporate the natural environment into their daily work lives." All of which, according to Becki McMinn, marketing coordinator for Arborguard, results in yet another and often overlooked benefit—better employee morale and retention.

In Houston, architect Fred Buxton began working with nature's envelope as early as the late 1960s. Buxton was commissioned to design an office park on land that was a virtually unspoiled coastal pine forest. Called the North Loop Office Complex, Buxton's plan recognized the importance of preserving both the canopy trees and the understory, which was composed of a variety of ferns and woodland wildflowers.

Unfortunately, as with many projects, ownership and management can change over the years, and the North Loop Office Complex is no exception. Once hailed as a significant landscaping milestone, it has strayed from Buxton's original vision. When I visited the property in 1994, I was greeted by crisply pruned hedges of red-tipped photinia and a St. Augustine lawn—a painfully conventional landscaping style in this part of the country. The grounds, which had once been lush with native Eastern Gulf Coast ground covers, ferns, and grasses, were now populated with Asian azaleas struggling in the local black clay (called gumbo) and an array of thirsty annuals such as vodka begonias and impatiens.

When I visited Buxton at his home, I asked him when he had last seen this office complex. "It's been at least fifteen years," he responded. "Don't go back," I advised him. "It will break your heart."

Ownership and management changes over the years have resulted in a deviation from architect Fred Buxton's original envelope vision. While most of the conifers still remain, most of the native vegetation has been replaced by lawns and exotic flora. An important element in creating envelope developments, be they commercial or residential, is to establish covenants that will assure that the concept is maintained in the future.

In most cases, people using the envelope concept preserve the natural surroundings, but sometimes the habitats no longer exist and must be recreated. Because only 0.5 percent of our original prairies still exist, those who desire landscapes that reflect this precious heritage must turn to prairie restoration—planting and nurturing the native grasses and forbs (flowering prairie plants) that had once grown so abundantly in the locale.

The Sears world headquarters in the Prairie Stone Business Park in Hoffman Estates, Illinois, is such a restored habitat, incorporating both prairie and wetland sites, woodlands, and nature trails. The 200-acre campus was designed as a low-maintenance, naturalistic prairie meadow that would blend in harmoniously with the surrounding area. Even better, it provides a corridor linking two other wildlife areas, thus enlarging wildlife habitats instead of fragmenting them.

Union Gas is the local gas utility in Brantford, Ontario. Their four-and-a-half-acre prairie garden was laid out by MacKinnon, Hensel, and Associates of Waterloo. A natural wetland of sedge and cattail was extended. The environmental design, installation, and organic maintenance are by Jeff Thompson of Kitchener. This landscape gets lots of public exposure because many customers come here to pay their gas bills. The landscape was planted in June 1995, replacing an overworked cornfield. The soil is three feet of sand over clay pan. The first plant to bloom was partridge pea, which had not been seen in the area for sixty years. It had not been planted, so the seed must have been lying dormant in the soil. Each summer for the first two years, 150 hours of weeding were required. Jeff estimates that the construction-installation costs were 60 percent that of a lawn, and the maintenance is 100 percent for the first four years. Then it drops to 15 percent—a big savings for the long term.

The main offices of Union Gas in Brantford, Ontario, has a 4.5-acre restored prairie that greets employees and customers.

The Fermi National Accelerator Laboratory (FermiLab) is another showcase for successful prairie restoration. Under the direction of Robert Betz, retired biology professor from Northeastern Illinois University, 1,030 acres of 6,800 acres of old farmland have been planted in prairie. At first, maintenance engineer Bob Lootens and the other groundskeepers who were in charge of planting and maintaining the prairie were highly skeptical. As Lootens put it, "I grew up as a dairy farmer, and he was asking us to plant weeds on a good corn crop!" But Betz had good people skills as well as technical know-how. Now Lootens is a prairie advocate. "These forbs and grasses are as long-lived and impressive as an oak tree," he says. "Everyone knows it's a crime to cut down an oak. It's as big a crime to plow a prairie." The members of the grounds crew no longer see weeds; they see a hundred rare species, and they wish they could spend more of their time on seed gathering, burning, and other prairie activities. They burn spring and fall each year, rotating to different areas so everything gets burned once every two years.

The Lady Bird Johnson Wildflower Center (formerly the National Wildflower Research Center) was founded in 1982 by former First Lady Lady Bird Johnson and was dedicated to the preservation and reestablishment of our country's indigenous flora. Today, that dedication is focused more sharply than ever at the center's new facility, which was opened to the public in April 1995 and now draws over 100,000 visitors a year.

Located on 179 acres of beautiful Hill Country real estate southwest of Austin, Texas, the $9 million center is a model of environmentally correct construction techniques as well as water-conserving landscaping. The planning, design, and construction of the center took over five years, and the emphasis was always on

A sea of goldenrod adorns the grounds of the Fermi National Accelerator Laboratory in Batavia, Illinois. Here 1,030 acres are devoted to restored prairie.

The envelope was employed in building the Lady Bird Wildflower Center in Austin, Texas. The live oak woodlands surrounding the main campus were fenced off for protection, and individual trees bore price tags ranging from $2,000 to $25,000 to assure that they would not be injured during construction.

creating a facility that was not merely functional but aesthetically pleasing and environmentally sensitive.

One of the distinguishing features of the center is a network of aqueducts and cisterns designed to collect, store, and reuse rainwater—the largest rooftop rainwater harvesting system in the country. Another is the choice of building materials; the limestone, sandstone, cedar, pecan, and oak are all native to the region. They were selected because they required minimal transporting, thereby conserving fossil fuels, as well as for their architectural qualities.

Don Walker, director of the Conway School of Landscape Design, where landscape architecture is taught along with an understanding of ecological concerns.

A CHANGE IN EMPHASIS

Most laypeople are amazed to learn that students of landscape architecture are exposed to very little plant information during their schooling. The typical curriculum devotes less than 10 percent of classroom time to the flora that will compose the designs they will create; the remaining class time is devoted to hardscaping: installing lighting, erecting retaining walls, laying out and constructing walkways and irrigation systems—that sort of thing. What consideration is given to plants is invariably limited to conventional nursery stock; native plants are rarely if ever touched upon.

Little wonder then that the vast majority of landscaping projects that come from these landscape architects has little to do with nature and almost always reflects the controlled, formalized, high-maintenance style seen around residences and corporate headquarters from coast to coast.

Happily, that is changing, albeit slowly. Among the handful of institutions combining environmental studies with their landscape architecture curricula are the University of Georgia, the University of Michigan, and Syracuse University. One of the best examples of this change in emphasis can be seen at the Conway School of

Landscape Design in Conway, Massachusetts. Here, students are offered a ten-month master of arts program in site design and land use planning that has at its core a true sense of respect for the natural environment.

Students come to this sleepy New England village from all over the world (Germany, Canada, Japan, and Brazil) to study and work within this close-knit learning community. The school structure itself reflects the intimacy of the experience, being in a converted house and barn. John Martin, professor of landscape architecture at the University of Massachusetts, says he was attracted to "the human scale" of the school and to a curriculum that "rejects glitz and gimmicks to concentrate on the fundamentals of landscape architecture, providing a practical means for combining sound design and conservation."

The program is structured around professional-level work for residential, municipal, and nonprofit organizations, and it combines all the requisite technical know-how of their profession with a strong emphasis on understanding and accommodating natural systems. Toward this end, students are given a basic knowledge of geology, climate, soils, hydrology, botany, wildlife, and other natural sciences, as well as specific skills in engineering, construction, planning, and conservation. They are also exposed to some of the finest minds in this and related fields through a series of guest lecturers who come to Conway to share their insights. Over the years these lecturers have included ecologists Henry Art and Bill Niering, graphic designer Mike Lin, environmentalist Paul Rezendes, and solar engineer Steven Strong, as well as some of the leading landscape architects and designers in the country, such as Darrel Morrison, Carol Franklin, and Michael Hough.

Founded in 1972, the Conway School operates under the direction of Donald Walker, who came to the faculty in 1978 after fifteen years of teaching undergraduate and graduate courses at the University of Illinois and Ball State University, in Muncie, Indiana. An award-winning landscape architect in his own right, Walker has a passionate commitment to the natural world, and he insists that his students must fully understand the ecological consequences of their work.

To assure that the center would be built in harmony with nature, a botanical survey was conducted early on, giving all parties concerned a thorough understanding of the plant and wildlife communities existing at the site. In addition, a geological and hydrological study was made so that the specific recharge features of the Edwards aquifer, situated beneath portions of the center, would be known and taken into account. A bubbling "mountain pool" situated in the main pavilion—a feature that attracts children as pollen attracts butterflies—will one day be fed by the aquifer and will serve as a barometer for the health and well-being of that sensitive regional water resource.

The architectural firm of Overland Partners of San Antonio, the master site planner, Darrel Morrison of the University of Georgia, and the landscape architect, J. Robert Anderson of Austin, were all given the same basic request: blend the land and the buildings in a complementary and harmonious manner. "If a conflict arose between the buildings and the land," says David Northington, former executive director of the center, "the land always won."

An example of this land-first thinking is the fencing that separated the building activities from the natural landscape surrounding the center. Trees within the live oak and juniper woodland were carefully marked for preservation and were assessed a dollar value based on trunk and branch dimensions. Tags were then attached to the trees with prices ranging from $2,000 to $25,000. If any member of a contractor's crew damaged a tree, the cost of the damage would be deducted from their boss's payment. In addition, over 250 plants were rescued from construction zones and later transplanted to other areas during the landscaping phase.

~ Obstacles and Opportunities ~   11

In January 1999, I was asked to speak at the National Association of Home Builders (NAHB) annual convention being held in Dallas. The National Wildlife Federation had invited me to share the two-hour time slot they had been assigned on early Sunday morning. We were to speak on "creating backyard and community wildlife habitats," and the envelope concept fit in perfectly. Because of the early hour and the fact that this was the first time a presentation on this topic had ever been offered at this convention, we expected a small turnout; we figured that if we got ten people in the audience we'd be lucky. In fact, over sixty builders and developers showed up.

Waiting for my turn at the dais, I suddenly realized that this would be the first time I would be giving my presentation to professional builders, and they just might take offense at my comments about bulldozers leveling the landscape. In fact, I had long held the belief that developers ought to be viewed not as a problem but as an opportunity, and I have met many who are very environmentally aware.

I also felt some kinship with this gathering because my father, who had been a civil engineer, had once been involved in new home construction, supervising a 200-home development in New Jersey back in 1948–1949. In those postwar boom

"Someday, all this will be infrastructure."

times, nobody was saving trees or thinking about the environment; in fact, that particular subdivision was built on the site of a defunct nursery, so there wasn't anything to preserve.

Still, as I stepped up to the microphone, I felt as vulnerable as a distillery owner speaking at an AA meeting. I needn't have worried. The question-and-answer session following my talk was one of the best I'd ever had, and I learned a lot. One builder actually thanked me for not blaming his profession for high-density housing. "That's more a matter for Planned Parenthood than us," he quipped. Another stated that many developers he knew wanted to build more environmentally but were confronted by mountains of red tape and local building codes that made this next to impossible.

Tree ordinances dictate the location and size of the shade trees on a property, and often perfectly healthy specimens have to be cut down to conform to these mandates. Nearby wetlands have to be drained despite the negative repercussions to wildlife. Excessively wide roadways and easements are required, shaving off chunks of property that might otherwise be left intact with native vegetation. I was told of an ordinance in Maryland (happily now defunct) that demanded that a ten-foot-wide flat mowed area be established all around a house. I learned of other codes that made it illegal to collect rainwater, use "gray" water, or have understory vegetation—all environmentally sound practices.

Other ordinances required that the property be reshaped so as to provide "proper drainage" away from the house, in many cases destroying the indigenous vegetation and the natural topographical features that help give the property its character.

These restrictions come about not because builders want them—often such ordinances mean added expense and trouble—but because legislators enact them to meet real or perceived problems. The intentions may be good, but the necessary information to create environmentally sound codes is not available or even sought out. Input from the general public, which is woefully ignorant on environmental matters, is often the impetus behind some of these ordinances. Code enforcers cannot change existing regulations. Even when they are sympathetic to the builders who want to do the right thing, they can do nothing.

Michael Pawlukiewicz at the Urban Land Institute in Washington, D.C., is very vocal about what needs to be done. His research and educational organization is dedicated to collaborating with all factions in the construction industry and to bringing a sense of reasonableness into play. "We study the goals or aims that inspired the regulations in the first place," he says. "Then we look at how those same goals can be achieved in an environmentally friendly way. And then we ask legislators, if the same ends can be achieved through environmental methods, wouldn't that be okay?"

Calling this "smart growth," Pawlukiewicz stresses that "it's vital that we develop a greater flexibility in dealing with these situations. It shouldn't take two or three years for an environmentally oriented builder to get special approvals for his plans; time, after all, is money, and he'll get discouraged and either wind up going along with the existing methodology or he'll decide to build elsewhere.

"We also have to get away from the 'quick-fix' approach involved in enacting these codes," he adds. "These regulations will have impact on future generations, and they need to be looked at."

Recently I was shown an excellent example of how a local building code worked to destroy land rather than preserve it. The site was in Santa Fe, New Mexico, in a part of the community called the "escarpment district." Here, the intention of the code writers was admirable: to prevent construction atop the ridgelines, thereby protecting the view of residents across the way from public rights of way. Moreover, the codes forbade construction on any land with a slope of twenty degrees or more. The only place on this particular site that was deemed buildable, according to the city's codes, was at the bottom of the property, even though this necessitated cutting a highly visible Zorro-like zigzagged driveway down the precipitous slope to the building site. Worse, because it had been cut through the piñons and junipers growing on the escarpment, chopping off almost half of their feeder roots, most of these trees flanking the driveway would very likely die within a year or two—creating an even worse eyesore. Thus a building code that was designed to protect the view resulted in more destruction to the landscape than building the house in a more elevated location.

According to local building codes, the house could only be built at the bottom of this steep grade to protect the ridgeline. But this necessitated putting in a zig-zag road down to the site, harming the root structure of numerous trees flanking the road. This driveway and the trees that would undoubtedly soon start to show signs of stress—perhaps even die—will create a far greater eyesore than a house at the top ever would.

"The city should have been more flexible," said the architect who showed me the site. "They should have allowed construction on the slope up closer to the top, and saved the trees and the view." Building there was certainly possible, he said, pointing out that the ground was very stable. "If building codes like this had existed in San Francisco, that city would never have been built," he pointed out.

What he suggested was a system that gives credits to a builder for finding other, more environmentally sensitive means to achieve the same ends. If a builder could amass a specified number of credits, then the codes could be eased somewhat. Credits can be earned by planting new vegetation, preserving established vegetation, installing "invisible" roads and driveways, or building aesthetically pleasing screening walls that blend in to the landscape, for example, using the same kind of rock found on the site.

Revegetating with native flora should be a part of any such system. I have seen developments that are presented as "environmentally correct" but are in fact terribly misguided. One developer went to a great deal of trouble and expense to plant hundreds of screening trees on the slopes around his homes. Most of them were not native to the area; a number of riparian trees that need continual irrigation were interspersed with drought-tolerant native trees, and they all shared the same drip system. Bad enough, but a number of highly invasive Russian olives were also spotted on this site. Interestingly, this particular development is touted by the city as an example of what an ideal subdivision ought to look like.

Ultimately, the public needs to recognize the importance of living on environmentally friendly land, both for themselves and for wildlife. Legislators need to understand the long-term repercussions of their laws, and developers need to realize that environment-friendly homes are becoming increasingly attractive—and marketable—to a growing segment of the population. And they have to be more willing to work to change restrictions that tie their hands.

I can think of no more effective way to encourage developers to build envelope homes than for *local municipalities to levy lower property taxes on environmentally friendly homes* in much the same way that landowners get agricultural tax exemptions. It just seems logical: homes that conserve water and electricity, while at the same time offering the added benefits of habitat renewal and reduced pollution, deserve favored treatment over conventionally built and landscaped homes that are a continual drain on municipal and environmental resources.

After consulting with the NAHB, the National Wildlife Federation, and various state, county, and municipal agencies, I have been unable to locate any community that offers such a tax break, including environmentally friendly towns such as Southlake, Texas; Long Grove, Illinois; and Aspen, Colorado, where progressive tree ordinances and building codes have been enacted allowing for sensible weed ordinances and naturescapes close to homes and businesses. Some states are now offering tax breaks to landowners for conserving large tracts as wildlife habitats, although they restrict any building on the property.

Perhaps the most frequent comment I hear concerning the envelope is, "Well, sure, the envelope makes sense if you have three or four acres, and you're building homes in the $500,000 and up category. Clearly the envelope isn't feasible for middle-class residential developments."

True, the majority of examples I've come across have been in "pricey" master-planned communities. But I have also seen several individually built homes in the $200,000 range. Careful planning and low-cost land made preservation of much of the natural surroundings possible. But in large-scale high-density developments, with homes priced below $200,000, the environmental response will be, more often than not, a case of restoration rather than preservation.

In many cases, natural areas (preserved or restored) within a high-density development can be achieved by creating joint or shared habitats; where four backyards come together, a small woodland or other habitat can be saved or re-created, affording more privacy for the homeowners and viable habitats for wildlife. Homeowners are also encouraged to revegetate with indigenous plants on the rest of the property. In some other developments, green spaces are a part of the overall master plan—one lot of natural habitat for a certain number of homesites.

John L. Knott Jr., who developed Dewees Island in South Carolina, is developing several high-density subdivisions with homes priced below $100,000. In one case, the 127-acre property is abandoned farmland; the only remaining indigenous vegetation is a fringe of woodland, which is marked for preservation. The rest of the community will be revegetated with native plants appropriate to the site. The homes themselves will be built with the latest energy saving designs, materials, and appliances. Called sustainable development, this approach makes the most efficient use of human, natural, and capital resources. "Building in harmony with the environment," Knott explains, "is less expensive than dominating or destroying natural resources. Since all resources are limited, this practice contends that man can be a resource provider, not just a resource user."

An important part of controlling capital outlay, says Knott, is preplanning that can reduce infrastructure costs from 40 to 60 percent. "Let's say I doubled the cost of the planning phase," he says. "That's a drop in the bucket compared to the cost of the infrastructure itself. We builders are trained to think incrementally. We see things in little boxes. We know from past experience that this phase should cost so much, that phase should cost this much. But we have to learn to think holistically, considering the overall development. This means bringing a new flexibility to our work." Builders, he contends, are the most creative resource in a community, displaying great entrepreneurial spirit. It's a flexibility that Knott believes most of his colleagues will understand and adapt to.

Civano, in Tucson, Arizona, is another exciting example of how a moderately priced development can be designed as a sustainable development, integrating some 2,600 homes—ranging from $90,000 to $200,000—and 1 million square feet of commercial space with state-of-the-art resource efficiency and ecologically responsible land management. Civano's developers are committed to making this a xeriscapic community, recommending only drought-tolerant native plants for use in both home and commercial landscapes. Moreover, homes will have two water systems, one for potable water and the other utilizing reclaimed rainwater and household (gray) water for nonedible plant irrigation.

Thirty percent of the 1,145-acre site is preserved as natural desert, while indigenous vegetation from other areas are being salvaged and replanted. So far over 2,400 cacti and ground covers and 465 mature trees have been successfully transplanted, exceeding plant preservation guidelines set down by the city of Tucson. Utilizing new techniques for salvaging mature trees, Civano has achieved an unprecedented success rate of 97 percent. Restoration plans also call for revegetating areas on the property that have been damaged due to overgrazing. In addition, programs are in place for permaculture, rainwater harvesting, and reuse of reclaimed water.

Driving to Civano to meet Kevin Kelly, president of the development company, I couldn't help noticing several nearby subdivisions in various stages of completion; they were all being built along conventional lines. I asked Kelly what it will take to bring other builders into line with the ideals exemplified at Civano. "Our

Civano is no cookie-cutter subdivision. A number of local builders are bringing their own special styles here and blending them into the overall vision. The landscaping in front of this model is newly planted but will soon spread into a lush xeriscapic display that will be sustained by a separate reclaimed water system.

Aside from salvaging many native plants from the property and keeping them on drip systems until they are replanted on the property, Civano maintains its own nursery that grows a variety of drought-tolerant plants for use in both residential and commercial landscapes within the community.

success," he responded without hesitation. "People are buying here at a remarkable rate. The home-buying market is changing. It's going our way. Each year some 2 million homes are built, and 98 percent are still assembly line conventional construction. But people are seeing what we're doing here—and what a few other builders and developers are doing around the country—and they're liking it because it makes sense and it's achievable at affordable prices. They like the way we tread lightly on the land and use our natural resources wisely. They like how we take advantage of the free solar capital available here. And they like the sense of true community that exists here. The more the public sees of this approach, the more they'll be expecting other developers to provide the same kind of living environment. Conventional approaches just aren't going to cut it in the new century."

Mississippi landscape architect Robert Poore also preaches the gospel of sustainable rather than traditional maintainable developments, and he contends that landscape ecology must be a viable force within the discipline of landscape architecture. "In the past," he says, "many landscape architects have ignored basic ecological principles, and instead pursued high-image design at the expense of natural systems."

Today, he says, it is becoming increasingly important for designers and developers to take into account what Pennsylvania landscape architect Carol Franklin calls processes and patterns. In a world faced with dwindling resources, Poore maintains that it is no longer enough for builders to understand the techniques of construction alone. "We need to understand the environmental, biological, and ecological functioning of all the components of the ecosystem we're building in," he says, "including how food chains operate, the importance of species diversity, and seasonal effects on wildlife and flora."

One environmentalist stated that we have no more than a hundred years to "turn things around. After that it will be too late." Others think that is an optimistic viewpoint. The fact is, we no longer have the luxury of taking our natural surroundings for granted. Admittedly, building inside nature's envelope is not a cure-all; our environmental problems are vast and multifaceted, and there are many fronts on which we must fight this battle, not the least of which is learning to control our soaring world population, which is the root of virtually all our other environmental problems.

Still, as long as we must build, we must do so with increasing concern for our surroundings. Carol Franklin described three basic steps to responsible development: "First, if there is any existing natural habitat on the site, we preserve it and the systems that support it. Second, if there is disturbed or damaged habitat on the site, we fix it and manage it. Third, if an opportunity exists to reestablish a habitat that once existed, or could exist on the site, then we reestablish it."

In our new century, we'll be better off if these become the guiding principles for us all.

Appendix:
Information
Resources

Native Plant Societies, Arboreta, and Related Organizations (addresses and area codes subject to change)

ALABAMA

Alabama Wildflower Society
240 Ivy Lane
Auburn AL 36830

The Birmingham Botanical Gardens
2612 Lane Park Rd.
Birmingham AL 35223
205-879-1227

ALASKA

Alaska Native Plant Society
P.O. Box 141612
Anchorage AK 99514-1613
907-333-8212
akkrafts@alaska.net

Georgeson Botanical Garden
University of Alaska
West Tanana Drive
P.O. Box 757200
Fairbanks AK 99775-7200
907-474-5651

ARIZONA

Arizona Native Plant Society
P.O. Box 41206
Sun Station
Tucson AZ 85717
anps@azstarnet.com

Arizona-Sonora Desert Museum
2021 N. Kinney Rd.
Tucson AZ 85743
520-883-2702

Mountain States Wholesale Nursery
10020 West Glendale Ave.
Glendale AZ 85307
602-247-8509

ARKANSAS

Arkansas Arboretum
Pinnacle Mountain State Park
11901 Pinnacle Valley Rd.
Roland AR 72135
501-868-5806

Arkansas Native Plant Society
Dept. of Math & Sciences
University of Arkansas
Monticello AR 71655
870-460-1165 or 870-460-1066
sundell@uamont.edu

California Native Plant Society
1722 J Street, Suite 17
Sacramento CA 95814
707-882-1655
www.cnps.org

The Living Desert
47900 South Portola Ave.
Palm Desert CA 92260
760-346-5690

Rancho Santa Ana Botanic
   Garden
1500 North College Ave.
Claremont CA 91711
909-625-8767

Santa Barbara Botanic Garden
1212 Mission Canyon Rd.
Santa Barbara CA 93105
805-682-4726

Society for Pacific Coast Native
   Iris
977 Meredith Ct.
Sonoma CA 95476

Southern California Botanists
Dept. of Biology
Fullerton State University
Fullerton CA 92634
714-278-7034
aromspert@fullerton.edu

Theodore Payne Foundation
10549 Tuxford St.
Sun Valley CA 91352
818-768-1802
theodorepayne@juno.com

Colorado Native Plant Society
P.O. Box 200
Fort Collins CO 80522

Kenilworth Aquatic Gardens
1900 Anacostia Ave. SE
Washington, D.C. 20020
202-426-6905

Florida Native Plant Society
P.O. Box 6116
Spring Hill FL 34611-6116
813-856-8202

Atlanta Botanical Garden
1345 Piedmont Ave.
Atlanta GA 30309
404-876-5859

Georgia Native Plant Society
P.O. Box 422085
Atlanta GA 30342
770-343-6000
HDeV@juno.com

National Tropical Botanical
   Garden
P.O. Box 340
Lawai, Kauai HI 96765
808-332-7324

Idaho Botanical Garden
2355 N. Penitentiary Rd.
Boise ID 83712
208-343-8649

Idaho Native Plant Society
P.O. Box 9451
Boise ID 83707
www2.state.id.us/fishgame/in
   psi.htm

Grand Prairie Friends
www.prairienet.org

Illinois Native Plant Society
20301 E. 900 N Rd.
Westville IL 61883
217-662-2142
ilnps@aol.com

Lincoln Memorial Garden and
   Nature Center
2301 East Lake Dr.
Springfield IL 62707
217-529-1111

Southern Illinois Native Plant
   Society
Botany Dept.
Southern Illinois University
Carbondale IL 52901

Hayes Regional Arboretum
801 Elks Rd.
Richmond IN 47374-2526
765-962-3745

Indiana Native Plant &
    Wildflower Society
5952 Lieber Rd.
Indianapolis IN 46228-1319
812-988-0063
pharstad@topaz.iupui.edu

IOWA
Des Moines Botanical Center
909 East River Dr.
Des Moines IA 50316
515-242-2934

Iowa Prairie Network
P.O. Box 516
Mason City IA 50402-0516
www.netins.net/showcase/blue
    stem/ipnapp.htm

KANSAS
Cimarron National Grassland
242 East Hwy. 56
Elkhart KS 67950
316-697-4621

Kansas Wildflower Society
R.L. McGregor Herbarium
2045 Constant Ave.
Lawrence KS 66047-3729
785-864-5093
c-freeman@ukans.edu

KENTUCKY
Kentucky Native Plant Society
Dept. of Biological studies
E. Kentucky University
Richmond KY 40475
606-622-2258
http://157.89.1.144/bio/jones/
    knps.htm

Land Between the Lakes
Tennessee Valley Authority
100 Van Morgan Rd.
Golden Pond KY 42211

LOUISIANA
Louisiana Native Plant Society
R.R. 1, Box 151
Saline LA 71070

Lafayette Natural History
    Museum
637 Girard Park Dr.
Lafayette LA 70504

Society for Louisiana Irises
1812 Broussard Rd. E.
Lafayette LA 70508
318-856-5859

MAINE
Wild Gardens of Acadia
Acadia National Park
P.O. Box 177
Bar Harbor ME 04609
207-288-3338

MASSACHUSETTS
The Conway School of
    Landscape Design
46 Delabarre Ave.
Conway MA 01341-0179
413-369-4044
info@csld.edu

New England Wild Flower
    Society
180 Hemenway Rd.
Framingham MA 01701-2699
508-877-7630
www.newfs.org

MARYLAND
Chesapeake Audubon Society
Rare Plant Committee
P.O. Box 3173
Baltimore MD 21228

Maryland Native Plant Society
14720 Claude Ln.
Silver Spring MD 20904

MICHIGAN
Fernwood Botanic Garden
13988 Range Line Rd.
Niles MI 49120
616-695-6491

Wildflower Association of
    Michigan
3853 Farrell Rd.
Hastings MI 49058
616-948-2496
marjif@iserv.net

MINNESOTA
Minnesota Landscape
    Arboretum
University of Minnesota
3675 Arboretum Dr.
Chanhassen MN 55317-0039
612-443-2460

Minnesota Native Plant Society
220 Biological Science Center
University of Minnesota
1445 Gortner Ave.
St. Paul MN 55108
651-773-9207
mnps@altavista.net
www.stolaf.edu/depts/biol-
    ogy/mnps

MISSISSIPPI
Mississippi Native Plant Society
111 North Jefferson St.
Jackson MS 39201
601-354-7303

MISSOURI
Center for Plant Conservation
Missouri Botanical Garden
P.O. Box 299
St. Louis MO 63166-0299
314-577-9450

Missouri Native Plant Society
P.O. Box 20073
St. Louis MO 63144-0073

The Missouri Prairie
    Foundation
Box 200
Columbia MO 65205
www.moprairie.org

Shaw Arboretum
P.O. Box 38
Gray Summit MO 63039
314-577-5142

MONTANA
Montana State University
    Arboretum
W College Ave. and S. 11th Ave.
Bozeman MT 59717
406-994-5048

Montana Native Plant Society
P.O. Box 992
Bozeman MT 59771

NEBRASKA
Homestead National Monument
Route 3, Box 47
Beatrice NE 68310
402-223-3514

Prairie/Plains Resource
    Institute
1307 L St.
Aurora NE 68818
402-694-5535
ppri@hamilton.net

NEVADA
Desert Demonstration Garden
3701 W. Alta Dr.
Las Vegas NV 89153
702-258-3205

Mojave Native Plant Society
8180 Placid Dr.
Las Vegas NV 89123

Northern Nevada Native Plant
    Society
P.O. Box 8965
Reno NV 89507-8965

NEW JERSEY
Tourne County Park
53 E. Hanover Ave.
Morristown NJ 07962-1295
973-326-7600

New Jersey Native Plant
    Society
Cook College, Office of
    Continuing Education
P.O. Box 231
New Brunswick NJ 08903-0231

NEW MEXICO
Living Desert Zoo and
    Gardens
1504 Miehls Dr.
Carlsbad NM 88220
505-887-5516

Native Plant Society of New
    Mexico
P.O. Box 5917
Santa Fe NM 87502-5917
505-454-0683

NEW YORK
Cooperative Sanctuary Program
Audubon International
46 Rarick Rd.
Selkirk NY 12158
518-767-9051

Brooklyn Botanic Garden
1000 Washington Ave.
Brooklyn NY 11225
lorigold@bbg.org
www.bbg.org

NORTH CAROLINA
North Carolina Native Plant
    Society
900 West Nash St.
Wilson NC 277893

NORTH DAKOTA
Gunlogson Nature Preserve
Icelandic State Park
13571 Hwy. 5 West
Cavalier ND 58220
701-265-4561

OHIO
Ohio Native Plant Society
6 Louise Dr.
Chagrin Falls OH 44022
inkys@juno.com

Wegerzyn Horticultural
    Association
1301 E. Siebenthaler Ave.
Dayton OH 45414
937-277-9028
www.dayton.net/MetroParks

OKLAHOMA
Oklahoma Native Plant Society
2435 Peoria Ave.
Tulsa OK 74114

Oxley Nature Center
6700 E. Mohawk Blvd.
Tulsa OK 74115
918-669-6644

OREGON
Native Plant Society of Oregon
2584 N.W. Savier St.
Portland OR 97210
503-248-9242
www.teleport.com/non-
    profit/npso/

Natural Areas Association
P.O. Box 1504
Bend OR 97709
541-317-0199
naa@natareas.org

PENNSYLVANIA
Bowman's Hill Wildflower
    Preserve
Route 32, River Rd.
New Hope PA 18938
215-862-2924

Brandywine Conservancy
    Wildflower and Native Plant
    Gardens
Route 1
Chadds Ford PA 19317
610-388-2700

Shenk's Ferry Wildflower
    Preserve
9 New Village Rd.
Holtwood PA 17532
717-284-2278

RHODE ISLAND
Rhode Island Native Plant
    Society
P.O. Box 114
Peace Dale RI 02883

SOUTH CAROLINA
South Carolina Native Plant
    Society
P.O. Box 759
Pickens SC 29671
864-878-1786
tgoforth@innova.net
www.scnativeplants.org

Wildflower Alliance of South
    Carolina
P.O. Box 12181
Columbia SC 29211
803-799-6889

SOUTH DAKOTA
Great Plains Native Plant
    Society
P.O. Box 461
Hot Springs SD 57747
605-745-3397
cascade@gwtc.net

TENNESSEE
Tennessee Native Plant Society
227 E. Brushy Valley
Powell TN 37849

TEXAS
Chihuahuan Desert Research
    Institute
P.O. Box 1334
Alpine TX 79831

El Paso Native Plant Society
7760 Maya Ave.
El Paso TX 79931

Native Plant Society of Texas
P.O. Box 891
Georgetown TX 78627
512-238-0695
www.lonestar.texas.net/~jle-
    blanc/npsot.html

Native Prairies Association of
    Texas
3503 Lafayette Ave.
Austin TX 78722-1807
512-480-3059
www.sunsetc.com/npat/index.
    html

UTAH
Utah Native Plant Society
3631 South Carolyn St.
Salt Lake City UT 84106

Natural Resources
    Conservation Service
125 South State St., Rm. 4402
Salt Lake City UT 84138

VIRGINIA
Eastern Native Plant Alliance
P.O. Box 6101
McLean VA 22106

Virginia Native Plant Society
P.O. Box 844
Annandale VA 22033

WASHINGTON
NatureScaping Wildlife
    Botanical Gardens
11000 N.E. 149th St.
Vancouver WA 98682
360-604-4400

Washington Native Plant
    Society
P.O. Box 28690
Seattle WA 98118-8690
888-288-8022
wnps@blarg.net
www.televar.com~donew/
    wwnps.html

WISCONSIN
Society for Ecological
    Restoration
University of Wisconsin
    Arboretum
1207 Seminole Hwy.
Madison WI 53711
608-262-9547

Wehr Nature Center
9701 W. College Ave.
Franklin WI 53132
414-425-8550

WEST VIRGINIA
West Virginia Native Plant
    Society
P.O. Box 2755
Elkins WV 26241

WYOMING
Wyoming Native Plant Society
P.O. Box 1471
Cheyenne WY 82003

NATIONAL
Center for Plant Conservation
P.O. Box 229
St. Louis MO 63166
http://cisus.mobot.org/CPC

The Lady Bird Johnson
    Wildflower Center
4801 LaCrosse Ave.
Austin TX 78739
512-292-4200
www.wildflower.org

Native Plant Conservation
    Initiative
1849 C St., NW, LSB 204
Washington, D.C. 20240
202-452-0392
www.nps.gov/plants/coop.htm

National Wildlife Federation
8925 Leesburg Pike
Vienna VA 22184-0001
800-822-9919
www.nwf.org

The Nature Conservancy
1815 North Lynn St.
Arlington VA 22209
703-841-5300
www.tnc.org

The Wildlands Project
1955 West Grant Rd., Ste. 148
Tucson AZ 85745
520-884-0875

Wild Ones—Natural
    Landscapers, Ltd.
P.O. Box 23576
Milwaukee WI 23576
312-845-5116
www.for-wild.org

CANADA
Canadian Nature Federation
1 Nicholas St., Ste. 520
Ottawa ON K1N 7B7
www.magma.ca/~cnfgen

Canadian Wildlife Federation
2740 Queensview Dr.
Ottawa ON K1B 1A2
613-721-2286

The Evergreen Foundation
355 Adelaide St. West, no. 5A
Toronto ON M1V 1S2
604-689-0766
info@evergreen.ca

The Native Plant Society of
    British Columbia
2012 William St.
Vancouver BC V5L 2X6
604-255-5719

North American Native Plant
    Society
P.O. Box 336, Station F
Toronto ON M4Y 2L7

Tree Appraisals

American Council of
    Consulting Arborists
700 Canterbury Rd
Clearwater FL 34624
813-446-3356

Council of Tree and Landscape
    Appraisers
5130 W. 101st Circle
Westminster, CO 80030-2314

International Society of
    Arboriculture
303 West University
P.O. Box 908
Urbana IL 61801
217-328-2031

National Arbor Day
    Foundation
100 Arbor Ave.
Nebraska City, NE 68410
402-474-5655

National Arborists Association
P.O. Box 1094
Amherst NH 03031
603-673-3311

References

*Assessing the Benefits and Costs
    of the Urban Forest*, by J. F.
    Dwyer, E. G. McPherson, H.
    W. Schroeder, and R. A.
    Rowntree. *Journal of
    Arboriculture*, September
    1992.

Building with Nature (1996),
    booklet published by a multi-
    agency partnership, includ-
    ing Citizens for Greenspace,
    Indiana Urban Forest
    Council, and the School of
    Public and Environmental
    Affairs at Indiana University.
    P.O. Box 814, Carmel IN
    46032.

*A Guide to Developing a
    Community Tree Preservation
    Ordinance* (1995),
    Department of Natural
    Resources, Division of
    Forestry, 500 Lafayette Rd.,
    St. Paul MN 55155-4044.

Guide for Plant Appraisal (8th
    ed., 1992), available from the
    International Society of
    Arboriculture, P.O. Box GG,
    Savoy IL 61874.

Trees Make Sense, by Elizabeth
    Brabec. Scenic America, 21
    DuPont Circle, NW,
    Washington, D.C. 20036.

Bibliography

Ajilvsgi, Geyata. *Butterfly Gardening for the South*.
Dallas: Taylor Publishing, 1990.

Amos, Bonnie B., and Frederick R. Gehlbach, eds.
Edwards Plateau Vegetation: Plant Ecological
Studies in Central Texas. Waco, Tex.: Baylor
University Press, 1988.

Barbour, Michael G., and William Dwight Billings,
eds. *North American Terrestrial Vegetation*. New
York: Cambridge University Press, 1988.

Barry, John M. *Natural Vegetation of South Carolina*.
Columbia: University of South Carolina Press,
1980.

Begley, Sharon. "Aliens Invade America!" in
Newsweek, August 10, 1998.

Bergon, Frank ed. *The Wilderness Reader*. Reno:
University of Nevada Press, 1994.

Bormann, F. Herbert, Diana Balmori, and Gordon T.
Geballe. *Redesigning the American Lawn: A Search
for Environmental Harmony*. New Haven: Yale
University Press, 1993.

Brooklyn Botanic Garden. *Going Native:
Biodiversity in Our Own Backyards*. Edited by
Janet Marinelli. Brooklyn, N.Y.: Brooklyn
Botanic Garden, 1994.

Buchmann, Stephen L., and Gary Paul Nabhan. *The
Forgotten Pollinators*. Washington, D.C.: Island
Press, 1996.

Clarke, Gilliam. "Desalination: Wave of Our Future for
Water Needs." *St. Petersburg Times*, May 25, 1998.

Cundiff, Bred. "Lands for Life." *Wildflower
Magazine*, Summer 1998.

Daniels, Stevie. *The Wild Lawn Handbook*. New York:
Macmillan, 1995.

Daugherty, James. *Henry David Thoreau: A Man for
Our Time*. New York: Viking, 1967.

Druse, Ken. *The Natural Landscape*. New York:
Clarkson N. Potter, 1989.

——. *The Natural Habitat Garden*. New York:
Clarkson N. Potter, 1994.

Duncan, Wilbur H., and Marion B. Duncan. *Trees of*

the Southeastern United States. Athens: University of Georgia Press, 1988.

Erickson, Jon. *Ice Ages: Past and Future*. Blue Ridge Summit, Pa: Tab, 1990.

Fantle, Will. "Why Johnny Can't Breed." Isthmus, August 5–11, 1994.

Gill, Brandan. *Many Masks: A Life of Frank Lloyd Wright*. New York: Putnam, 1987.

Gleason, Hendy A., and Arthys Cronquist. *Manual of Vascular Plants*. 2d ed. Bronx, N.Y.: New York Botanical Garden, 1991.

Gore, Al. *Earth in the Balance*. New York: Houghton Mifflin, 1992.

Graham, Alan. *Late Cretaceous and Cenozoic History of North American Vegetation*. New York: Oxford University Press, 1999.

Graves, William, ed., "Water: The Power, Promise, and Turmoil of North America's Fresh Water." *National Geographic*. Special ed., November 1993.

Gould, Frank W. *Grasses of the Southwestern United States*. Tucson: University of Arizona Press, 1951.

Hollingsworth, Craig, and Karen Idoine. "An Environmental Gardener's Guide to Pest Management." In *The Environmental Gardener*. Handbook no. 130. New York: Brooklyn Botanic Garden, 1992.

Hoose, Phillip. *Building an Ark: Tools for the Preservation of Natural Diversity Through Land Protection*. Covelo, Calif.: Island Press, 1981.

Jenkins, Virginia Scott. *The Lawn: A History of an American Obsession*. Washington, D.C.: Smithsonian Institution Press, 1994.

Kaufmann, Edgar Jr. *Fallingwater*. New York: Abbeville, 1986.

Knopf, Jim, et al. *Natural Gardening*. Berkeley Calif.: Nature Company, 1995.

Kruckeberg, Arthur R. *Gardening with Native Plants of the Pacific Northwest*. Seattle: University of Washington Press, 1982.

Lemire, Robert A. *Creative Land Use: Bridge to the Future*. Boston: Houghton Mifflin, 1979.

Metcalf, C. L., and W. P. Flint. *Destructive and Useful Insects*. New York: McGraw-Hill, 1928.

Moore, Ann. "Rock House Finds Bedrock of Support." *New Mexico Magazine*, May 1999.

Orr, Oliver H., Jr. *Saving American Birds*. Gainesville: University Press of Florida, 1992.

Ottesen, Carole. *The Native Plant Primer*. New York: Harmony Books, 1995.

Pests and Diseases. Time Life Books. Complete Gardener Series. Alexandria, Va, 1995.

Randall, John M., and Janet Marinelli. *Invasive Plants: Weeds of the Global Garden*. Brooklyn N.Y.: Brooklyn Botanic Garden Publications, 1996.

Ring, Elizabeth. *Henry David Thoreau: In Step with Nature*. Brookfield, Conn.: Millbrook, 1993.

Robinson, Scott K. "The Case of the Missing Songbirds." *Consequences* 3, no. 1 (1997).

Rudofsky, Bernard. *Architecture Without Architects*. New York: Doubleday, 1964.

Sauer, Leslie. *The Once and Future Forest*. New York: Island Press, 1998.

Sexton, Richard. *Parallel Utopias: The Quest for Community*. San Francisco: Chronicle Books, 1995.

Sharp, Curtis W., George A. White, and James A. Briggs. "The Plants That Followed People." In *Our American Land: 1987 Yearbook of Agriculture*. Washington, D.C.: USDA, 1987.

Simpson, Benny J. *A Field Guide to Texas Trees*. Houston: Gulf, 1988.

Steger, Will, and Jon Bowermaster. *Saving the Earth*. New York: Alfred A. Knopf, 1991.

Thoreau, Henry David. *Walden*. 1854. Reprint, Boston: Beacon, 1997.

Van Zandt, Roland. *The Catskill Mountain House*. Hensonville, N.Y.: Black Dome, 1993.

Wasowski, Sally, and Andy Wasowski. *Requiem for a Lawnmower*. Dallas: Taylor, 1992.

———. *Gardening with Native Plants of the South*. Dallas: Taylor, 1994.

———. *Native Landscaping from El Paso to L.A.* Chicago: NTC/Contemporary, 2000.

———. *Native Texas Plants: Landscaping Region by Region*. 2d ed. Houston: Gulf, 1997.

"Water Challenges." Editorial. *Jerusalem Post*, June 3, 1998.

Weck, Egon. "In Harmony with the Land." In *Mid-Atlantic Country*, November 1987.

Winslow, Susan, producer. *The Power of Water*. Aired on PBS, November 10, 1993.

Wovcha, Daniel S., Barbara C. Delaney, and Gerda E. Nordquist. *Minnesota's St. Croix River Valley and Anoka Sandplain: A Guide to Native Habitats*. Minneapolis: University of Minnesota Press, 1995.

Index

Morrison, Darrel G., 76, 125
Mulching, 82–83

Nash, John, 50
Natural Garden, The (Druse), 18
Natural landscape, 17
  legal challenges to, 22
  preserved, 17–18
  trend toward, 22–23
  weed laws and, 20–22
Natural zone, at building site, 63
  fencing of, 65, *66*
Nature
  19th century idealization of, 49–50
  detachment from, 8–10
  ignorance of, 6
"Nature" (Emerson), 50
Nature's envelope, xv–xvii, 11,
  architect/builder selection for, 61
  author's experience building in, 85–94
  house placement in, 61–64, *63, 64*
  marking zones of, 64–66
  misconceptions about, 55
  plants and, 56–61, 67–68, *69,* 71–74
  see also Green development
Nelson, Ron, 70
North Loop Office Complex, 120, *121*
Northington, David, 22–23, 125
Norway maple, 59
Nurseries, 60, 81

Oaks, 31
Once and Future Forest, The (Sauer), 29

Organic mulching, 82–83
Ornamental trees, 31–32, *32*
  in Pacific Northwest, 37
  in Texas, 39
Overland Partners, 125

Pacific Northwest, 37
Parallel Utopias (Sexton), 99
Park Mesa Condominiums, 117, *118*
Pawlukiewicz, Michael, 129
Peel, Larry, 117
Penalties, for damage to site, 67–68
Peru, 48
Pesticides, 26–28
  advertisements for, 20
Pierson, Norah, home of, 47, *48*
Pines, 31
Piñon, 62, *79*
Plant survey, before building, 56–58
  conducting, 60–61
  weeds and, 58–60
Plants
  marking of, at building site, 64–66, *65*
  native, 14–15, 17, 81–82
  saving of, at author's site, 89–92
  value of, 67–68
Plater-Zyberk, Elizabeth, 105
Pollan, Michael, 104
Poore, Robert, 134
Population, loss of habitat and, 28–29
Portola Valley Ranch, Calif., 38, 100–102, *101*
Prairies, 35
Preserved landscape. *See* Natural landscape

Private zone, 63
Pruning, by builder, 91
Purple loosestrife, 35, 58, 59

Quack grass, 21, *21*

R-2000 Program, 116
Rabbitbrush, 42
Rainfall
  forest loss and, 26
  house placement and, 62, *62,* 82, 91
Rappaport, Bret, 22
Read, William A., 52
Reagan, Michael, 26
Recycling, for building materials, 116
Red oak scrub, *40*
Red spruce, 38
Residential development, in nature's envelope, 95–108, *96, 98, 101–103, 105–106,* 131–34, *133*
Ribbon markers, at building site, 65–66, *66*
Root cuttings, 82
Rosebay rhododendron, 32
Rosenberg, Susan, 120
Rosenfeld, Spence, 120
"Round-up ready" crops, 27–28
Rudofsky, Bernard, 48
Russian olive tree, 7, *7,* 58, 59

Salt lick, 73
Sandhills, 40–41
Sangre de Cristo Mountains, *4*
Sante Fe, N.M., building codes in, 129–30, *130*
Sauer, Leslie, 29
Savannas. *See* Shrubland, savannas, woodlands

Andy Wasowski is a freelance writer and photographer specializing in landscaping and environmental issues. His work has appeared in *Life Magazine, Audubon, Fine Gardening, Sierra,* and *Sunset.* He has also provided on-air commentary for National Public Radio's *Living on Earth.* **Sally Wasowski** is a nationally recognized landscape designer and authority on native flora. The Wasowskis have been honored for their work by the American Horticultural Society and the Canadian Wildflower Society. They are authors of several books, including *Gardening with Prairie Plants* (Minnesota, 2002).

Darrel G. Morrison, FASLA, is professor of environmental design at the University of Georgia.